Byron Martin Lelong

California Walnut Industry

Byron Martin Lelong

California Walnut Industry

ISBN/EAN: 9783337405441

Printed in Europe, USA, Canada, Australia, Japan

Cover: Foto ©Suzi / pixelio.de

More available books at **www.hansebooks.com**

CALIFORNIA

WALNUT INDUSTRY.

COMMERCIAL IMPORTANCE, LONGEVITY, POLLINATION, VARIETIES, PLANTING,
SOIL, PROPAGATION, BUDDING, GRAFTING, PRUNING, HARVESTING;
ENEMIES OF THE WALNUT, AND REMEDIES; AREA OF
WALNUT CULTURE IN STATE, IN AMERICA,
AND IN EUROPE, ETC.

By B. M LELONG,

Secretary State Board of Horticulture of California, and Chief Horticultural Officer.

Author's Edition, from Report State Board of Horticulture for 1895-6.

SACRAMENTO:

A. J. JOHNSTON, : : : SUPTERINTENDENT STATE PRINTING.
1896.

CALIFORNIA

STATE BOARD OF HORTICULTURE.

CONTENTS.

AN EIGHT-YEAR-OLD WALNUT TREE.
From the seed; being the age seedling walnut trees begin to bear.

THE WALNUT.

By B. M. LELONG,
Secretary State Board of Horticulture, and Chief Horticultural Officer.

(1) COMMERCIAL IMPORTANCE.

Holding a prominent place among the fruit products of California, stands the walnut. This position has been attained in the past few years, and is due to the results of experience—and many failures—which have shown the proper conditions under which this fruit will thrive, its requirements in soil, climate, and location, and the production of varieties adapted to the peculiarities of our State. The old-time saying that the area of walnut culture in the State "is very limited" and confined to any particular section, has, by happy chance, proved a fallacy, and is disproved by the numerous productive orchards that bear witness to its successful culture. While the early plantings were made in the southern counties, where the culture of the walnut is pursued with great magnitude, the industry is gradually spreading and broadening. While the walnut will withstand a very low temperature, it is very susceptible to sudden changes, and a hot day suddenly following a frosty night will chill the young wood, and often proves fatal to a young orchard, setting it back a season's growth. The same is true in the springtime on the opening of the flowers or catkins—a chill will frequently cause them all to drop and render the crop a failure. For this reason a location free from prevailing frosts, or one where the sun will not strike the trees until the effects of the cold have been overcome, is very desirable. The latter trouble can be largely overcome by planting some of the late-blooming varieties, which do not send forth their catkins until danger from frosts is largely past.

California walnuts are fast supplanting those from foreign countries. Only a few years ago the growers of these nuts here had a very hard struggle to introduce them, being obliged to accept the humiliating price of from 3 to 6 cents a pound less than that paid for imported walnuts. Gradually, however, a reduction came, in favor of the California product, and now Eastern dealers will take our best walnuts at prices equal to, and in many cases exceeding, those obtained for those coming from abroad. Our State affords a splendid field for the walnut industry, and although thousands of trees have been planted, and the acreage is being extended every year, it is believed that overproduction need not be feared. Our producers have all America for a market, and they are not slow to appreciate the advantages of their position.

(2) THE "ENGLISH" OR "PERSIAN" WALNUT.

The walnut (*Juglans* regia*, Linn.) is a native of Persia, and is supposed to have been introduced into our State by the Franciscan monks

---

*Juglans is a genus of trees consisting of six species; three are natives of the United States, viz.: *J. nigra*, or black walnut; *J. cinerea*, or butternut, and *J. fraxinifolia*, or ash-leaf walnut. The other three species are *J. regia*, "English" or "Persian" walnut; *J. pterocarpa* grows on Mount Caucasus, and *J. baccenta* in Jamaica and Spain.

during the establishment of the California Missions in 1769. Records of its early history are scant, but mention is made of walnut trees growing about the Missions by most of the writers of the "Record of the Founding of Missions," and the "History of Franciscan Missions of California," and, therefore, it is safe to assume that with the advent of the Missions dates the introduction of this valuable tree. In the Mission yards are yet to be seen walnut trees of those early plantings, and while age began to tell on these many years ago, they still live and bear nuts, but few in number and small in size.

* "When I first arrived in Los Angeles, in December, 1854, there were numerous small bearing 'English' walnut orchards and sundry isolated *large* trees which could not have been less than ten years old, and some of which must, I am confident, have been more than twenty-five (25) years old.

"In talking to-day with Mr. Stephen C. Foster, he fully corroborates my view, that the English walnut was first brought to Los Angeles, or to California, by the Missionary Fathers, or by individual laymen during the missionary era. Mr. Foster says that when he came here, in 1847, there were several large English walnut trees here, that he is certain were not less than twenty years old. One of these was on the old Pryor place, on Alameda Street, which I remember well, and another on the old Louis Vigne property, etc., which would make their planting extend back to 1827, or before. So that I think it would, without doubt, be historically true to say that the cultivation of the so-called 'English' walnut was commenced in California as early as the first quarter of this century (and possibly still earlier) by the Mission Fathers, or under their patronage and encouragement.

"It would have been a very easy and natural thing to do, for persons coming here by sea to have brought a few walnuts, and for the Friars to have planted some of them. What could have been more natural than for the priests or other officials, civil or military, who came from Spain, to desire to raise, in this fertile country and mild climate, all those useful fruits and food products that they were familiar with in their native land? We are all compelled to admire the practical forethought of the organizers of even the very first expedition in 1769, Galvez, Serra, etc., in this respect."

The most careful research as to the early walnut plantings has been made, showing that among the first walnut orchards of early history, planted outside of the Missions, were those of the late Col. J. J. Warner, in San Diego (supposed to have been planted in 1843, on a ranch named after him, and which name it still bears—"Warner's Ranch"), the Pryor, Vigne, Wolfskill, Dalton, Boyle, Shaw, Childs, and Briswalter orchards at Los Angeles, the Temple orchard at La Merced Ranch in the San Gabriel Valley, the Heath orchard at Carpinteria, and the Wilson and Kewen orchards at San Gabriel. A small planting was made in 1846, near Calistoga, by Frank E. Kellogg, Sr. The largest of these plantings are the Heath, Briswalter, and Temple orchards. The Briswalter is of most recent planting; the Heath orchard is the largest in the State of early history. It is impossible to ascertain the exact years these orchards were planted, as all the persons above mentioned (excepting Mr. Heath) have since passed away. These orchards are said to have been set out from 1850 to 1865; however, the only authoritative information I can find is the statements of several persons, whose minds are not clear as to the exact time.

† "In 1858, the year I obtained my walnut seed of Mr. Wolfskill, of Los Angeles, I had no knowledge of walnuts being planted in this State, except those planted by the Mission Fathers. The trees from which my seed was taken were planted by the Franciscan Fathers. The Wolfskill place, in Los Angeles, was an old garden of the Mission. Mrs. Wolfskill was a native Spanish lady of Los Angeles, and informed me that the vineyard and walnuts were bearing when she was a small child, in fact she did not know the age, they were large trees. Judging from the oldest trees I have at present, I think those walnut trees must have been over fifty years old in 1858. I made inquiry for walnut trees with the view of purchasing, and could not find any one who had tried their culture

* Letter from H. D. Barrows, a pioneer, February 29, 1896.
† Letter from Hon. Russell Heath, of Carpinteria, February 27, 1896.

except the Mission Fathers. I was advised to plant walnuts by Reverend Father Gonzalez, head of the Franciscan Missions, who resided for many years in Santa Barbara. From him I obtained much of its history taken from documents in his possession. The nuts were brought from Spain, first planted in Mexico, and taken from there to South America. The first planting in California was at San Diego; two at San Gabriel, Los Angeles County, three in Los Angeles. From my information, I think the Wolfskill place was one of the first planted in what is now the City of Los Angeles. After the Mission at Santa Barbara was established, there was a propagating garden established and seeds and plants brought from the Mission south. Father Gonzalez told me no walnuts were planted, but almonds were, but they were not considered a success and were abandoned, while the olive, grape, fig, pomegranate, and some other fruits were cultivated with great success. There was no record of the walnut having been planted north of the Mission of San Buenaventura, where I saw for the first time a walnut tree in 1852."

* "Father never spoke to me of the 'English' walnut orchard that was set out; but speaking to Don Ramon Valenzuela, who was in father's service in 1849, he said that in that year he plowed the orchard, and that then a few of the trees were commencing to bear. As you know how long it takes the trees to bear,† you can judge how old they were at the time. Don Miguel Pryor had just one walnut tree older than ours, but father was the only owner of an orchard at the said time."

‡ "I think Mr. Wolfskill's orchard (now dug up and land turned into streets and building lots) had been planted at least ten years at date of my arrival here, last of 1854, and Mr. Elijah Moulton is of the same opinion. Mr. Coronel, Colonel Warner, and Governor Pico would probably have known, but all three of them have died within the past two years. The Andre Briswalter walnut orchard of 1,000 trees must have been planted, I think, as early as the 60's, if not in the late 50's. J. R. Barton, Sheriff, had planted a walnut orchard on his ranch at Los Nietos River before he was killed by the bandits in January, 1857."

In almost every county of the State are found large walnut trees showing great age, planted very irregularly among other trees, indicating that no attempt had been made to produce a walnut orchard by itself, but were planted by the growers to experiment as to their growth and furnish walnuts for the table.

At Knight's Ferry, Stanislaus County, is a seedling walnut tree of enormous size, the property of Asa Collins, planted by W. E. Stewart in 1858. The seed was brought from France by a French sailor. Out of the three walnuts he brought only one grew, which is the parent tree of many plantings.

§ "In 1873, Mr. Finch, of Alameda, ordered from Messrs. Rose & Grant, of Topeka, Kansas, fifty trees of a so-called 'Persian' walnut, introduced by them from Persia, one year old, which sold for $10 each. The order could not be filled, so he only obtained thirty-six, of which Mr. Latham bought ten, Mr. Selby two, J. D. Roberts four, and Wm. Meek twelve. The sale of the balance was withheld."

¶ "Mr. D. C. Vestal has a walnut tree at San José, about sixty feet high, bearing medium thin-shelled nuts. The nuts from which this tree was produced came from Chile, and were planted about thirty years ago by Mr. Vestal, where the tree now stands. He has gathered from it yearly about a barrel of nuts."

In 1883, Mr. Kelsey, of Fresno, reported to the State Horticultural Society that he had at Fresno two trees of the so-called "English" walnut, that were then about six feet in circumference and about fifty feet high.

∥ "At Mud Springs, El Dorado County, are to be seen several large 'English' walnut trees."

In Winters, Solano County, at the John Wolfskill place on Putah Creek, are many large trees that yearly produce medium-size nuts of

* J. W. Wolfskill, letter of March 13, 1896.
† Trees of this so-called "English" walnut come into bearing at the eighth year from the planting of the seed; therefore, the orchard must have been set out about in 1841.
‡ H. D. Barrows, letter of March 14, 1896.
§ Pacific Rural Press, 1873, p. 193.
¶ Proceedings State Horticultural Society, April 27, 1883.
∥ Pacific Rural Press, 1871, p. 460.

fair quality; these, however, were grafted on the black walnut, and are
about thirty years old.

* "My father, F. E. Kellogg, settled in Napa Valley about midway between the present
towns of St. Helena and Calistoga, in 1846. In 1848 he planted some walnuts in his
nursery. When the trees were two years old (in 1850) he planted them about his door-
yard (ten or twelve in number), where some of them remained for more than forty
years. From time to time, father added to the number of his walnut trees, but never
planted a very large orchard of them. Some of the trees in my orchard here in Santa
Barbara County are from nuts taken from the old trees in Napa Valley."

The largest walnut orchard of early planting in the northern part of
the State is located near Los Gatos, in Santa Clara County; it is about
thirty years old, and produces fair crops yearly. The largest orchards
of recent planting are in Lake and Sonoma counties. In San Lorenzo,
on the Wm. Meck estate, is an extensive walnut orchard of early planting. In Sonoma, at the Vallejo place, and at Mission San José, are
many walnut trees that show great age and are healthy in appearance.
General Bidwell, at Chico, has a considerable number of walnut trees,
all vigorous and fruitful. Many such trees are to be found in Napa,
San José, Santa Clara, Merced, Modesto, Fresno, and Visalia. Along the
coast, in almost every county, are to be seen large walnut trees of early
planting. While these early plantings were small, and many consisted
· of isolated trees, as were those in the Mission gardens, yet those trees
mark a special epoch in the horticultural history of our State, as they
have proved the great longevity of the walnut, and enlightened the
growers as to their culture and future possibilities.

(3) LONGEVITY OF THE WALNUT.

The great and prodigious age attained by the walnut can only be con-
ceived from records of its early history. All the early botanical writers—
English, French, Italian—point out the fact that the walnut, in their
respective provinces, does not bear until it has reached the age of fifteen
to twenty-four years, and hardly becomes a paying investment until it
attains a prodigious age. In California, the walnut begins to bear at
the eighth year from the seed, and from that time on the crop increases,
and the orchards become remunerative. It is now not uncommon to see
walnut orchards from thirty to forty years old, in the prime of health,
producing every year bountiful crops.

† "In Persia, the tree comes into bearing at eight years from the planting of the seed;
in Italy, Spain, and the Island of Madeira, in about sixteen years; in France—the
southern part—in eighteen years; in England, in twenty-four years, and in California
in eight years, the same as in Persia. So, I take it, the southern part of this State is
nearest its home."

‡ "After fifteen or twenty years from the time of planting, the walnut gives only
hopes, so to speak, for its yield is yet so small that its value can hardly be reckoned; it
is only from thirty to sixty years that this tree can offer each year a product sufficient
to increase the income of the landlord. It takes a century, and over, before the wood is
good to be used in the arts."

§ "Walnut trees are spoken of that bear, in good years, 50,000 to 100,000 nuts; such
trees are truly very rare, and their trunks are not less than 15 to 20 feet in circumference."

* Frank E. Kellogg, of Goleta, letter of March 12, 1896.
† Hon. Russell Heath, in essay before Eleventh State Fruit-Growers' Convention, 1889.
‡ Maison Rustique, Vol. 2, Chapter XII.
§ Maison Rustique, Vol. 2, p. 143.

WALNUT BRANCH.
Showing development of male flowers, or staminate catkins, with the first period of growth two weeks before the appearance of the female flowers or pistillates.

WALNUT BRANCH.

Showing both staminate or male catkins and pistillates or female flowers in full bloom, having appeared together, or nearly so. The male organs or catkins emanate from the bud-cells in the axils of the leaves on twigs of the preceding summer, and the female flowers at the terminals of the new growth, with the embryo nuts.

THE WALNUT (*Juglans Regia*).   PLATE IV.

WALNUT BRANCH.

Showing male flowers or staminate catkins after blooming, and the female flowers or pistillates (and embryo nuts) above, just in bloom, having made their appearance two weeks later, and ready for fertilization.

* "In the village of Beachemwell, in Norfolk, may be seen a walnut tree (*Juglans regia*) which spreads its 'softly swelling hills' of leaves over the church-yard of All Saints Church, now in ruin, as if it sought to mingle leafy dust and human ashes. When this tree is arrayed in all its honors 'fresh and green' it is an object interesting by its symmetry and gigantic proportions. The crumbling walls of the ruin, throwing their shadow far away and standing out in gray relief from the green turf, beneath which the good forefathers of the village sleep in peace, offer a striking contrast to the huge mass of walnut foliage, presenting a specimen of its kind seldom equaled. This tree has produced in one season 54,000 nuts, and its dimensions are as follows: Circumference of the body of the tree near the ground, 32 feet; height of trunk, 10 feet; the circumference of the five large branches is 16 feet, 14 feet, 9 feet, 8 feet, 8 feet; the circumference of the extreme spread of the tree is 120 yards, and its estimated height is 90 feet."

† "On the road from Martel to Gramat (Lot) is to be seen a colossal walnut tree at least three hundred years old. The height of this tree is about 55 feet; its branches extend to a distance of 125 feet; the trunk, 14 feet in diameter, is only 20 feet high, but it sends out seven immense branches. It bears on an average each year 15 bags of walnuts."

‡ "An Italian architect mentions having seen at St. Nicholas, in Lorraine, a single plank of the wood of the walnut, 25 feet wide, upon which the Emperor Frederick III had given a sumptuous banquet. In the Baidar Valley, near Balaklava, in the Crimea, stands a walnut tree at least 1,000 years old. It yields annually from 80,000 to 100,000 nuts, and belongs to five Tartar families, who share its product equally."

(4) POLLINATION.

Until recent years no attempt was made to improve the varieties of the walnut in cultivation by cross-pollination, but the universal practice has been to plant the nuts selected from fruitful and rapidly growing trees, and the seedlings grown therefrom, on not becoming regular bearers, were dug up, as were also all trees producing inferior nuts. Trees producing nuts deficient in kernels were not uncommon, but were frequently reported, and many such trees still exist. From past experience it is readily to be seen how important it is for the grower to study and know the varieties, so as to plant and locate them in the orchard so that they may assist in the pollination of one another. In fact, the study of pollination becomes essential as the first step to successful fruit culture.

In all catkin-bearing trees—as the walnut—or of monœcious flowers, the flowers necessarily differ and have their sexes separated, but are borne by the same tree. The incoherent pollen is produced by the male flowers (pendulous green cylindrical catkins), which is distributed and comes in contact with the female flowers by the aid of insects, the air and wind, by fall of gravity, or by friction, thus insuring a crop. The male flowers, or staminate catkins, are the first to appear, and come out generally together with the first growth of the tree, although in many instances they appear before the trees put forth, but about the time they begin to show signs of growth. The female blossoms, or pistillates, appear much later, from one to three weeks intervening. In some of the European varieties the difference is very slight, the pistillates appearing about the time the staminates are in full bloom. Instances of this nature with the "English" walnut are very rare.

The male flowers, or staminate catkins, after blooming lose hold and drop, and, coming in contact with the limbs, thus distribute their pollen amongst the foliage of the trees. The pollen is also distributed and

* Gardener's Chronicle, London, 1857, p. 694.
† Gardener's Chronicle, London, 1852, p. 568.
‡ Gardener's Chronicle, London, Vol. VII, 1877, p. 310.

adheres to the limbs and leaves during the blooming period of the male catkins. . The fertilizing power of the pollen is not lost, but is preserved for an indefinite period, and a mere speck falling on the stigma of the female blossom is ample to render it fertile.

In many instances it has been observed that some trees will produce at times an abundance of flowers of one sex, and few or none of the other sex. Trees—as the walnut—that mature their pollen before the female flowers on the same tree are ready for fertilization, are called by botanists *proterandrous;* while others, called *proterogynous*, have their stigmas mature before the pollen is ready. The purpose of this curious functional difference obviously is in favor of cross-fertilization, by pollen, of flowers borne by other trees of the same species.

According to the Gardener's Chronicle, in 1888, reports became current of trees in portions of the walnut sections of France bearing a full crop, but the nuts failed to harden, the husks when about half grown withering up, and few good nuts were found. The kernels which were formed were soft and insipid. Reports made throughout were that "while there were plenty of nuts there was nothing in them," and after assigning different reasons for this failure, conclude "probably from imperfect fertilization of the flowers." Many other similar instances are reported as occurring in different groves.

* "It is a common occurrence for the walnut to be deficient in producing either the male or female blossoms, which it bears, both of which are essential to its producing and ripening nuts. I have a tree, now about twenty years old, which began a few years ago to show blossoms, but those merely female, without one male catkin appearing on the tree, and the consequence has been that after the flowers faded the fruit regularly dropped off. This season, there being a considerable show of female blossoms but no male ones, I thought of trying the plan followed by gardeners in the case of melons and other fruits where fertilization is not freely effected by nature, and having seen abundance of male catkins on a tree at a friend's, I asked him to send me some, and he accordingly sent me a small paper-bag full, which I dusted and threw over such of the female blossoms as were within my reach. The consequence has been that I now have about a dozen fine nuts, swelling out regularly, with every appearance of coming in due time into maturity. All the embryo fruit not fertilized have fallen off as usual. I am pleased with the success of my experiment, and mean, should my tree still prove deficient in male blossoms, with the assistance of my friend's, to supply its wants, and, by taking a little more trouble, I have no doubt I shall be able to render every female blossom fruitful."

As showing this curious functional difference in our own State, a few facts are cited. A nurseryman at Ventura observed a large seedling walnut tree, which, from its luxuriant growth and symmetrical form, he believed would be a variety worthy of cultivation. Accordingly, in the spring of 1886, he planted forty pounds of nuts gathered from that tree. When the seedlings bore, none of them produced nuts of any commercial value. This, of course, proved to be a sad disappointment to him, and, after waiting ten years for a crop, he dug up most of them. Some of the trees had become of large dimensions and had long, spreading branches, and were always quite full of nuts, but without kernels—all hull and shell. This functional difference was investigated; the trees were found to produce an abundance of flowers of the same sex, but few or none of the other, through which imperfect fertilization of the flowers the kernels in the nuts did not form—they were wanting. It is also interesting to note that no attempt was made to correct this curious phenomenon by artificial cross-pollination, by distributing pollen from staminate catkins, or male flowers, of other trees, before digging up the trees.

*Gardener's Chronicle, London, 1847, p. 541.

Through the continuous planting of the seed (as mentioned else-where), without regard to the laws of nature, has come about the degeneration of the species in many sections. Trees are frequently reported as having "never borne nuts"; others "bloom profusely, but are blooms of only one sex; the nuts have never set, and have become a barren waste." This is a summary of the reports that have been con-tinuously received for years past. In recent years more attention has been paid to the morphology of the walnut, and it is now better under-stood.

*"I have a few trees of the ordinary 'English' walnut. In 1878 the staminate blossoms came out in the latter part of March; they dropped off and perished on the ground. About the 15th of April the pistillates made their appearance. The result was the nuts dropped off. The next year the staminates made their appearance the 1st of April; they dropped off by the 10th, and between the 12th and the 15th the pistillates made their first appearance. The result was I had no walnuts. The next year, 1880, I found that the blossoming period came closer together, within a few days. About the 1st of April the staminate blossoms dropped off, and in a few days the pistillates began to make their appearance. I looked over the trees and found a few stunted staminate blossoms. I gathered them very carefully, and shook them over the trees. The result was that every tree over which I distributed the pollen was laden with walnuts."

Incidentally, I may mention that almond-growers were in a worse pre-dicament, and in many sections the culture of the almond was abandoned. The Languedoc, a variety first introduced, was found to produce an extraordinarily large number of flowers of one sex, and few of the other. The morphology of the almond was studied, with wonderful results, and many of these same localities are again planted to the almond, and are among the leading almond-growing sections of the State. It was also found that by planting different varieties in an orchard alternately, the pollen would intermix and aid in the setting of the fruit. This, however, was done in many cases without studying their blooming period, and consequently failure resulted. For instance, seedling trees of the bitter almond were planted in the orchard, as they were profuse bloomers, but the time of blooming was not considered. Seedling trees of the bitter almond are among the first to bloom, and put forth two weeks or more ahead of the standard varieties, so that when the latter came into bloom the pollen of the bitter almond had either been washed off by the early rains, or lost through other unfavor-able conditions, preventing its action on the other flowers. In order to accomplish the results aimed at, the varieties so intermixed must bloom together, or nearly so. I know of no instance where this has been tried on the walnut, but it is certainly worthy of trial, as it may tend to cor-rect this curious phenomenon, prevalent among some of our walnut orchards complained of, consisting of trees grown from seed. Of course, with the almond the experiment was much easier, because, after testing a certain variety, and its merits becoming fully known, they were repro-duced by budding. The long period required by the walnut to come into bearing was a bar to any experiments in this line, and it was grown from the seed almost altogether. But this is no longer so. Fruit cul-ture has reached the height of perfection, and is now being conducted on broad lines and scientific principles. Inferior seedlings are giving way to grafted and budded trees of the choicest kinds, or to seedlings of choice selection; their habits are studied, and the novice or the grower does not have to wait and undergo years of toil and anxiety to acquire

*W. H. Jessup, of Haywards, in essay read before State Horticultural Society, April 27, 1883.

results, but can profit by the experience of others who have made fruit culture the study of their lives, and who show their liberality and warmheartedness by sharing this knowledge with their neighbors.

(5) ORIGIN OF IMPROVED HOME VARIETIES.

While large walnut orchards were set out, and many new plantings made every season, consisting mainly of seedling trees produced from seed from the old historic trees of early introduction, no attempt was ever made to produce improved varieties by cross-pollination, and none are yet recorded. Only recently have improved varieties become known, and these originated from chance seedlings. In 1867, Mr. Joseph Sexton, of Goleta, Santa Barbara County, purchased in San Francisco a sack of walnuts supposed to have come from South America, labeled "English walnuts," from which he raised about 1,000 trees, and the spring following (1868) planted 200 of these trees in orchard form at Goleta. Sixty proved to be of a soft-shell variety. Later, he planted 24 trees raised from soft-shell nuts from his original trees; of this number 21 came true (the same) to the parent tree, and 3 made a much stronger growth, commenced fruiting in the sixth year, and produced a soft-shell nut, and an improvement over the original trees. The first he named "Santa Barbara Soft-Shell," and the latter "Improved Soft-Shell," by which names they are now known. In 1859, Hon. Russell Heath, of Carpinteria, furnished Mr. Stowe, at Santa Barbara, with a large quantity of walnuts from his orchard of so-called "English" walnuts, for planting. Among the trees that Mr. Stowe raised from that seed, one produced soft-shell nuts. It is Mr. Heath's firm belief that this nut must have come from a chance seedling produced by him from seed which he procured from the orchard of the late Wm. Wolfskill, at Los Angeles, from whom he obtained his first seed. There is no instance on record where any soft-shell walnuts had been produced prior to that time.

Mr. George W. Ford, of Santa Ana, originated soft-shell walnuts, which he christened "Ford's Eureka" and "Ford's Improved Soft-Shell." They were produced from seed grown by Mr. Sexton, of Goleta. Mr. Felix Gillet has originated the "California Paper-Shell," the "Columbus," the "Cluster Prœparturiens," and the "Mayette-Shaped Prœparturiens." Many other varieties have been catalogued, mostly because they were "new," but were never passed upon by any competent authority, or their merits determined. Most of these trees, on coming into bearing, produced a nut similar to that of the tree from which they originated as chance seedlings. These various types, not being distinctive enough to be classified by themselves, are all labeled "English walnuts."

WALNUT BRANCH.
Showing the mature nuts through the cracking of the husks, ready for harvesting.

FIG. 1.—Branch of walnut showing character of growth and an extraordinarily large amount of male, or staminate, catkins; reduced.

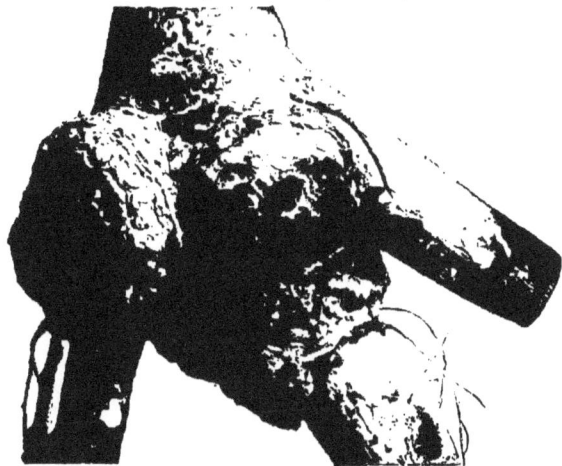

FIG. 2. -"Root knot" on young walnut.

(6) VARIETIES OF THE WALNUT (*Juglans regia*, Linn.).

ENGLISH.*

(Plate X, Fig. 2.)

Synonyms: Madeira, Naples, Los Angeles, Common, Chile, Mission, etc.

This walnut was the first introduced into our State; from it innumerable varieties have sprung, and of which the principal orchards of the State consist. The name is applied to any variety of the so-called "English" walnut. It would be difficult to determine the particular variety to which this name belongs; however, it is a name applied by common consent to any and all varieties that have originated from the so-called "English" walnut, and really is more of a commercial name through which the product is marketed.

The principal orchards of the State consist of trees grown from seed of the so-called "English" walnut, and while the walnut comes truer to seed than most fruits, it could not be claimed that *all* the orchards of the State are of this particular variety, simply because the trees were raised from seed of the original stock. In almost every orchard of the State of early planting are trees bearing nuts wholly unlike the nuts pro‹ duced by the parent trees, and they can only be classified as types of the original nut, showing the great variation produced from planting the seed. Many of these orchards, however, consist of types of rare quality, such as the orchards in the Los Nietos Valley, Santa Ana Valley, San Gabriel Valley, Carpinteria, Santa Barbara, etc. While most of the types that originated from the seed grown on trees of early planting · produced a hard-shell nut, there were many that produced a thin 'or soft-shell nut. The best and most productive orchards to-day consist of trees grown from seed of the original trees.

To describe the so-called "English" variety would be as difficult as to describe the seedling orange and its many types. Oranges cultivated from seed are known as "seedlings," but as the seed from these seedlings has been planted continuously, and though the trees so produced bear fruit so distinct and so variable, they are only *seedlings* from *seedlings*, and are accepted under that name without regard to variety.

Among those trees of early history were many that produced large, clear, hard-shell nuts, which were greatly sought in the market. The nuts of this type were in great demand for planting, although by continuous propagation from the seed for nearly a half century, without regard to the degeneration of the species, many of these types have been allowed to degenerate until their cultivation has been almost abandoned.

While seedling trees and small orchards of this so-called "English" walnut, or "Los Angeles nut," are met with in almost every county of the State, the successful culture of this nut and its many varieties has been confined to the lower counties—from Santa Barbara to San Diego. Trees grown from seed of this nut—"English"—in many sections have proved too tender to withstand the cold of winter and the heat of summer.

---

* For want of a better name, and to indicate the locality from whence it came (as it is supposed by all the earliest British botanical writers to have first been introduced into England by the Romans), it was called commercially the "English walnut."

They generally get cut back by frosts† in the spring, as they put forth too early to escape them. The trees keep growing quite late in the season, and the tender shoots and undeveloped growth suffer from the extreme heat, and are nipped by the frost in the fall.

Of late years several late-blooming varieties produced by chance have come into prominence, having most of the essential qualities required, and which are proving successful everywhere, and will hereafter, no doubt, supplant all others of this species.

While the walnut has reproduced itself, that is, "come the same," from seed, it has a tendency to revert to the wild state, as is the case with all trees when continuously propagated from seed. A variety can only be reproduced and remain constant by budding and grafting. In this State many such instances have been cited and recorded.

EUROPEAN VARIETIES.

The varieties described in this chapter have proved most promising of the numerous kinds introduced into our State in recent years. The descriptions given are by leading growers, whose opinions are worthy of fullest consideration:

Persian.—Generic commercial name, applied by common consent to all varieties of the *Juglans regia.*

* *Chaberte.*—(Plate XI, Fig. 9).—An old and most valuable variety; late in budding out. The nut is well shaped, roundish-oval, and of fair size; the kernel is of extra fine quality; good bearer. The Chaberte originated in France over a century ago, by a man named Chaberte, hence its name.

"The Chaberte is a good and thrifty variety."—West.

"The tree is very productive, developing its leaves and bloom *late* in the spring."—Rock.

* *Franquette* (Plate X, Fig. 5).—Blooms late in spring. Originated about the same time as the Mayette, in the southeast of France, by a man named Franquet. It is quite large, of an elongated oval, and very attractive; kernel full-fleshed and sweet, and of rich, nutty flavor. It also buds out late in the spring, being as hardy as Parisienne and Mayette. Very desirable as a market nut.

"Nuts very large and long; one of the finest for dessert."—Rock.

* *Mayette* (Plate X, Fig. 3).—This is one of the finest dessert and market nuts grown; it is quite large and uniformly so, well shaped, with a light-colored shell; the kernel is full-fleshed, sweet, and nutty. But what renders this valuable kind more valuable yet, is that it is very hardy, being late in budding out, which enables it to escape uninjured the disastrous effects of late frosts in the spring; it is also an abundant bearer. This is the nut imported into the United States under the name of Grenoble, but on account of duties to pay, and the nut being high-

---

* Described by Mr. Felix Gillet.

† On March 2, 1896, the northern and central portions of the State were visited by a severe frost and snowstorm. On the morning of the 3d I examined the growth of the English walnut in several orchards, which had already grown about 4 to 6 inches, and found much damage done to both the growth and the male catkins. The European varieties did not show any signs of starting. On March 15th the pistillates of the 'English" walnut made their first appearance, but all the male flowers, or staminate catkins, had dropped off. On March 22d the European varieties began to put forth. As a consequence there was no crop of "English" walnuts, but the European varieties set well.

priced in its home in France, a common and cheaper grade is often mixed with it, to the disgust of nut importers in New York and Chicago. The Mayette was originated by a man of the name of Mayet, one hundred and thirty years ago, having ever since been a great favorite as a market nut.

"My trees did not produce until the sixth year. They are a large, excellent nut."—West.

"One of the finest dessert nuts grown; large, full-fleshed, and sweet. Very late in budding, thereby escaping injury from late frosts."—Rock.

*Mesange.—This nut has a very thin shell, and derives its name of Mesange from a little lark of that name that goes to the kernel through the tender and thin shell; very productive. This may be regarded as a first-class family nut, but I would not recommend it as a market nut, on account of its rather small size and thinness of shell.

* Vourey.—This new and valuable variety of recent introduction originated near Vourey, France, hence its name. The nut has the shape of the Mayette, but is more round and smaller; the shell is thin, light colored, and smooth, and the kernel exceedingly sweet and nutty; very hardy.

"The nuts are very large and the shell well filled with a sweet, rich kernel. The leaves and flowers are produced late."—Rock.

Grenoble (Plate XI, Fig. 5).

*Meylan.—A new and very attractive variety, originated near the little village of Meylan, in the walnut district of France. The nut is of fair size; the smoothest one of our collection, very thin shell, and of excellent quality; buds out late.

*Scrotina (St. John) (Plate XI, Fig. 3).—I find this variety not to be so late in budding out as to not be sometimes injured by late frosts in the spring. The nut is of medium size, well shaped, with a very sweet, nutty meat; enormously productive.

"This variety came into bearing the fifth year from planting. It is of less value than others grown by me. Its flavor is not quite so delicate, and the shell a trifle harder, but as it is a week later in showing leaf in the spring, it will suit frosty localities."—West.

" Leaves and flowers of this variety are not developed until all danger of frost has passed; very productive."—Rock.

Mobart (Plate XI, Fig. 2).

* Vilmorin, or Cross-Bred.—This curious variety was obtained by "hybridizing" years ago, in France. It is a cross between the English walnut and the Eastern Black walnut, and was called Vilmorin after the leading member of the well-known seed firm of Vilmorin, Andrieux & Co., of Paris. The nut is small, and has the shape of the English walnut, but the furrows of the Black walnut; it is darker than the English and lighter than the Black. It can hardly be called an improvement on the Black walnut; surely it is not on the English. It is a very odd sort, having no commercial value whatever. We have fruited this cross-bred walnut for the last seven years, and find that either as a family or market nut this cross-bred variety is entirely worthless. It must be regarded and propagated, therefore, simply as an ornamental variety.

* Weeping Walnut.—A new and very curious kind of walnut, highly ornamental, the branches drooping down like those of the weeping-wil-

* Described by Mr. Felix Gillet.

low. We have had limbs on some of our weeping walnuts growing to eight feet through the summer, drooping straight down, with the ends dragging on the ground, and even trailing on it to a length of twelve to twenty inches. The nut is of fair size, oblong, thin-shelled, and of good quality. It looks to be a very abundant bearer.

Rivera Hard-Shell (Plate XI, Fig. 7).

Rivera Soft-Shell (Plate X, Fig. 8).

Laciniated, or Ash-Leaved.—The foliage of this kind of walnut is so delicate, so finely cut up, that it makes of it a most graceful ornamental tree, worthy to be planted conspicuously in the garden or front yard. The nut, besides, is exceedingly pretty, of fair size, round, with a very smooth shell and sweet kernel. The tree is claimed to be an abundant bearer.

Parisienne.—Large, excellent, starts late in spring. This beautiful nut, also one of the finest for dessert and market, was originated in the southeast of France, and not in the neighborhood of Paris, as its name would imply ; its beauty made it called *Parisienne*, in honor of the capital of France. The nut is large, broader at the small end than the Mayette and Franquette, and has a very pretty shape. It is as late as the Mayette, and as desirable for market.

"A most beautiful nut; one of the largest and best for dessert, broad and large, with full-fleshed kernel. Bears early and regular."—Rock.

Alpine, or Wonder of the Alps.—A new and very rare variety originated not long ago in the Alps Mountains, in France. Next to the Mammoth it is the largest walnut grown on my place. Though the shell looks a kind of rough, it is perfectly soft and thin, and the meat sweet and filling well the shell.

Lanfray.—A newly originated variety. Very pretty nut, oval in shape, of fair size and first quality.

Poorman.—A new kind, of recent introduction.

Fertile (Plate XI, Fig. 1).

Præparturiens or Fertile, First Generation.—This variety was introduced into the State by me, in the winter of 1870–71, and in my grounds, 2,600 feet up in the Sierra, are the first trees of that kind that ever produced fruit in this State. Described as follows: The Præparturiens was originated in France, in 1828; from the fact that it first bore nuts while being but two years old, the Latin name of Præparturiens was given to it from *Parturiens*, bearing, *Præ*, before—bearing before the usual time. It was also called Fertile, on account of its surprising fertility. The nut is small, though thin-shelled, and very sweet ; it is this nut that produces "Second Generation" trees.

Præparturiens or Fertile, Second Generation.—The Second Generation Præparturiens, the kind we recommend to plant, has retained all the characteristics of the original, only the nuts are much larger, and larger, too, than those of the third and fourth generations, seventy-five per cent of the trees bearing nuts from medium to large, and twenty-five per cent from small to medium, and of all sorts of shapes—all, however, being thin-shelled and of first quality. The Præparturiens is one of the most productive kinds, and bears heavy crops from the start, and it may be regarded as the best variety of walnut to plant for family use ; the largest Præparturiens nuts, though, being well marketable.

*Described by Mr. Felix Gillet.

Third Generation Prœparturiens.—The kind mostly sold in California under the generic name of Prœparturiens, and grown from nuts borne on Second Generation trees. The nut is generally small—too small for market, but of first quality.

Mammoth Prœparturiens.—A large-fruited variety of Prœparturiens, originated in France. The nut is extraordinarily large; soft shell, and with a full-fleshed kernel.

Prœparturiens (Plate XI, Fig. 8).—"This variety has proved exceedingly satisfactory. It will bear in nursery rows when not more than four feet high, and continue to have a crop every year, and has never been injured by spring frosts. On my place are seedlings of the second and third generations, which still convey their fertile and early-bearing qualities. The nuts on mature trees are of good size and of the best quality."—West.

Gant (Syn. *Bijou*) (Plate XI, Fig. 4).—"Nuts very large, twice or three times larger than the common walnut, and sometimes square or oblong in shape."—Rock.

"The Bijou is the largest walnut known. This variety began to bear when it had been planted four years, and has constantly increased its yield. In 1890 it bore a large crop, and in 1891 it set its fruit so quickly that I thought best to remove at least one third of it. The reputation of this tree in its home—France—is that of a shy bearer. The quality is excellent, superior to anything I have seen."—West.

Mammoth, or Jauge.—This is an immense nut, the largest yet originated. So large is the shell of some of them that "ladies' companions" are made out of the shells by fancy-goods manufacturers wherein to stow away gloves and handkerchiefs. The nut, though of such large dimensions, has a thin shell, and the kernel is of first quality.

Cluster (*Juglans Racemosa*) (Plate X, Fig. 7).—This remarkable kind of walnut, introduced some twenty years ago into this country, is a worthy rival of the Prœparturiens for productiveness, but superior for the beauty of the nuts. It derives its name of *Juglans racemosa* from the Latin word *racemosus*, meaning abundant in clusters, full of clusters, which is the main characteristic of that most beautiful variety. The nuts, when the tree is in full bearing, grow in long clusters of 10, 15, and even 25 to 28 nuts. The Cluster, like the Prœparturiens, reproduces itself well enough from the seed, *provided* that the nuts be gathered from trees *grafted from the original.* The nut is thin-shelled, of fair size, hermetically closed, with a smooth, white shell; in fact, a perfect beauty.

Barthere.—"A singularly shaped nut, elongated, broad at the center, and tapering at both ends; the shell is harder than that of other sorts."

Kaghazi.—Of doubtful origin; grown about Niles, in Alameda County.

Grand Noblesse.—Described, in "Nut Culture in the United States," as having originated by L. L. Bequette, of Los Nietos, but is very little known by the growers of that section.

VARIETIES OF HOME ORIGIN.

The chapter on pollination of the walnut illustrates how varieties originate by accident, or from chance seedlings. The following varieties originated in that way; they have been fully tried and their merits have become known, and are therefore entitled to be placed among the list of varieties worthy of cultivation:

* Described by Mr. Felix Gillet.

2—W

California Paper-Shell (Plate X, Fig. 1).— Originated by Mr. Felix Gillet. A nut borne on a grafted Chaberte, the tree being, therefore, a Second Generation Chaberte. The nut is only of medium size; shell very thin and almost white; kernel full-fleshed, exceedingly sweet and nutty.

Columbus.—Originated by Mr. Gillet. Produced from a Second Generation Mayette. The nut is very large, exceedingly pretty, roundish, with smooth, light-colored shell, and kernel of first quality. Named Columbus in honor of the World's Fair in 1893, the year that my second trees of that kind went into bearing.

Mayette-Shaped Præparturiens.—Originated by Mr. Gillet, some twenty-five years ago. A large nut, sitting on its end like the Mayette, hence its name. Full-fleshed kernel of first quality; heavy bearer. Solely propagated by grafting.

Cluster Præparturiens.—A variety of Præparturiens said to be very fine, also originated by Mr. Gillet. Nut large, oblong, smooth surface, perfect soft-shell; kernel fine and sweet. Growing in clusters.

Soft-Shell.—Originated from seed, by Mr. Joseph Sexton, of Goleta, Santa Barbara County, in 1868. The seed he procured in San Francisco, which was labeled "English," and was supposed to have been imported from Central America. Mr. Sexton describes this variety thus: "Nut looks very much like the imported Chile walnut, having the shape and color. The objection to this variety is that as the trees grow older the nuts grow smaller—diminish in size—and are not as salable as larger nuts."

Improved Soft-Shell (*Santa Barbara Soft-Shell*) (Plate X, Fig. 10).— Originated by Mr. Joseph Sexton, of Goleta, Santa Barbara County, in 1870, from seed of the "Soft-shell," crossed with the hard-shell or "English" walnut. The nut in outer appearance resembles the "English" or hard-shell, but the shell is as thin as the "Soft-shell," and the kernel or "meat" is a beautiful white color. Tree productive, uniform, and symmetrical in growth.

Ford's Improved Soft-Shell (Plate X, Fig. 6).—Originated in 1877 by Mr. George W. Ford, of Santa Ana, from seed he obtained in San Francisco, and supposed to have come from Mr. Joseph Sexton, of Santa Barbara. Out of the twenty-five pounds of walnuts he obtained, one hundred of the largest and finest nuts were picked out, and from these twenty large nuts selected. These were planted, and from which originated this "new" improved nut. The nut resembles the "Soft-shell." It is a large, clear nut, separates easily; the meat is very white, and the tree is a handsome grower.

Ford's Eureka (Plate XI, Fig. 6).—Originated by Mr. George W. Ford, of Santa Ana, from soft-shell nuts procured from Mr. Joseph Sexton, of Goleta. The nut is almost round, meat white, and very fine. Tree vigorous, and a fine grower.

ORIENTAL VARIETIES.

Among the most beautiful trees are the Japanese walnuts. Two varieties are known in this State, one (*J. Sieboldiana*) being grown for more than twenty years. While it has been grown successfully, its

*Described by Mr. Felix Gillet

economic importance has not as yet been determined. The nuts differ greatly from the varieties of *J. regia*, and present curious forms; they are, nevertheless, valuable, for the kernel is oily and sweet. The tree is very handsome, requires no pruning, is a strong grower, and very symmetrical in form, which, with its large, glossy leaves, of extraordinary size, render it most beautiful and especially suited for roadways and avenues. The tree is also valuable for stocks, as they "take" easily and are always healthy and of thrifty growth.

Japanese (Juglans Sieboldiana, Maxim) (Plate X, Fig. 4).—This variety has been cultivated very successfully in this State for more than twenty years. It is a beautiful ornamental tree, indigenous to Japan. The leaves are of enormous size. The nut is small and elongated, quite hard, but with a sweet kernel; of very little commercial importance.

Heart-Shaped (Juglans Cordiformis, Maxim).—This variety is also indigenous to Japan, and of recent introduction. The tree is similar in appearance to *J. Sieboldiana*. The nut is small and "heart-shaped," with a sweet kernel, said to be easily extracted by boiling for five minutes and then cracking.

Chinese (Juglans Mandshurica, Maxim).—This nut is also of recent introduction, and is indigenous to eastern Asia. Resembles closely the Eastern butternut in habit of growth and foliage, and is said to resemble it in the form and appearance of the nut.

(7) PLANTING, SOIL, AND OTHER REQUIREMENTS.

There is considerable difference of opinion among growers as to the proper age to plant walnut trees in orchard. Many contend that trees of three years' growth are best, while others contend that the seed should be planted where the tree is intended to grow, that it should never be transplanted, as in doing so certain roots, and especially the tap-root, have to be cut, which is detrimental to the growth and fruiting qualities of the tree. Others hold this practice to be a fallacy, and contend that the tree should be grown in the nursery until the sixth or eighth year, as is practiced in some countries.

*"I commenced transplanting trees in my nursery at one year old ; each year I renewed my nursery rows, planting each year so as to enable me to have trees for my own land, which I was obliged to clear in order to prepare it for the orchard. I planted after the first year, and after the second year, and continued planting year by year, from these different nurseries of different ages. When I arrived at the ninth year of planting, my trees had then been in bearing one year in the nursery. The trees that I planted out one year will bear fruit the seventh year. Eight years is as soon as I ever had them bear in my orchard from the seed. My experiments proved that the first or second year is an unnatural time to transplant the walnut. Why? There are two periods that the walnut ought not to be transplanted, that is, the second and after the fifth year ; the root starts the second year and makes a partial growth, and then it divides itself between top and root. The walnut will start and grow in root the first year without starting at the top, until it has made a certain period of growth, and then the root grows if not forced. I can force a walnut and make it grow ten feet the second year, but I say that is an unnatural growth and it ought not to be indulged in. The second year I say, then, is dangerous ; it is the period between the top and the root, and when you take it up you destroy that growth. The third year it makes top alone, comparatively no root ; it is then that your little tree, twelve inches high, grows up to the height of six to twelve feet. It is the top that it is making that year, and of course you do not desire to transplant a tree that is all to top and not to root, because when you take it from the nursery rows you must allow that tree to go down and make the root first, before it can make the top. After the third year you can transplant it with safety. Why? It has made

*Hon. Russell Heath, of Carpinteria. (Remarks apply to varieties of the "English" walnut, hard and medium shell nuts.)

its top. The fourth year its tendency is to root and not to top, because the fourth year it makes its spurs two inches on the side of that growth of the third year. The tendency of that year is all root, and if you want to transplant a young tree, then take up your three-year-old tree and transplant it and you will get your fruit then as quickly as the age of the tree will allow it to bear. After the fifth year, their tendency is not to make root; then is the time when those little branches two inches long send out the long arms to the distance of seven or eight feet; then it is that your tender shoots, especially in exposed conditions, are liable to be cut upon the end by the frost; then it is, if you are in the interior, that one hot blast will kill the ends of your trees, because it will have vigorous growth growing after the fifth year, and about the sixth, and the only remedy is the knife, because then the tree is touched by either cold or heat.

"Transplanting walnut trees, my experience is that I never had a nut from my trees that I transplanted from one year old to seven, without waiting six years. The best success I have had, and which plan I have followed, has been when I have transplanted trees in orchard form after they had passed the age of bearing in my nursery rows. I transplanted eight hundred eleven-year-old trees and did not lose one in transplanting. It does not cost much to cultivate trees for such a period in the nursery—a thousand can be cultivated in a day—and if they were in orchard the expense would be very great; and while the cost of transplanting trees at this age is probably ten times more than for three-year-old trees, you save more than ten times that amount in the cost and care through those years while in orchard."

* "I have raised trees from the seed and transplanted all the way from a year old up to six; and while they have grown and done well, I prefer to move them at three years of age, or about that time. The best trees that I have were transplanted at three years old."

† "I want one-year-old walnut trees one to three feet, two-year-olds four to six feet, and three-year-olds seven to nine feet, all of the above to be good stocky trees. The root of a three-year-old walnut is but a little longer than a one-year-old, though it is certainly larger. Of course, the root will grow in proportion to the top of the tree, for when a walnut commences to branch—which is about four years from the seed—then the root will commence to throw out laterals."

‡ "The usual custom is to set out two-year-old trees. In setting out young trees they should be inclined toward the coast or prevailing winds, and in trimming always try to keep them in that position. By using these precautions, and insisting on having the tap-root left at least three feet long when the trees are dug in the nursery, you will be likely to have your orchard in good shape when it is grown."

§ "The best aged tree to plant is two years old; not that I think the age makes any difference, but the trees at that age are of a size that they can be seen, and run no risk of getting damaged while being cultivated. In careful hands, I believe one-year-old trees as good or better, and perhaps it would be better still to plant the seed where you want the orchard trees to grow, but if planted in this way great care must be taken for two years in cultivating, that they do not get trodden down and the tops broken off, which makes the orchard uneven and unsightly. When planting two-year-old or larger trees, they should be selected, planting the largest trees first, and keep on doing so until the orchard is finished. By so doing you can get trees of equal size together. Some say it will not do to plant the seed where you want the tree to grow, that it must be transplanted, and the tap-root cut to make it fruit. I have tested this claim and found it a fallacy, and find that nuts planted alongside of one-year-old trees have produced prolific crops, and are larger trees than those one year older."

¶ "The plan of propagation is to plant the nut in nursery form in the spring of the year, in well-cultivated, sandy loam, about six inches deep. The first year they will grow from six inches to one foot high; the second, from one and a half to three feet; the third, from five to six feet. At this period it is considered the best for transplanting to permanent sites."

The walnut does best on a moist, warm, sandy loam, well under-drained. It is a very vigorous grower, and requires ample root room, vertically and horizontally, and unless this is furnished the tree will not do well. Soil, therefore, which has a hardpan near the surface, heavy clays, or soils which hold too much moisture, are to be avoided. A fairly light, friable loam, of good depth and easily worked, offers perfect conditions in the matter of soil for the walnut.

---

* O. N. Cadwell, of Carpinteria. (Also refers to varieties of the "English" walnut, or hard-shell nut.)
† George W. Ford, of Santa Ana. (Remarks apply to improved varieties on the "English" walnut, or soft-shell nuts.)
‡ A. Dorman, of Rivera, with reference to hard, medium, and soft-shell nuts.
§ Joseph Sexton, of Goleta, with reference to improved varieties of the "English" walnut, or soft-shell nuts.
¶ Hon. Ellwood Cooper, of Santa Barbara, with reference to varieties of the "English" walnut, or hard and medium-shell nuts.

At a recent convention of walnut-growers, the consensus of opinion as to the best soil for the walnut was in favor of a rich, deep, sandy loam, affording good drainage, and from 16 to 18 feet to surface water. This, however, met with opposition from some growers, who claimed to have attained equally good results with walnuts growing in soils principally adobe and with copious irrigation. It was also claimed that a rich alluvial soil, with a slight mixture of adobe, with water about from 15 to 20 feet from the surface, was one of the best and strongest soils for the walnut. Mr. Ford, of Santa Ana, has some twenty-year-old walnut trees very thrifty and bearing heavy crops every year, in land where the surface water is only 3 feet below; but time can only determine how long they will thrive under such conditions.

* "The walnut should be planted for profit and best results on deep, rich loam, with no hardpan, stiff clay, or impenetrable soil nearer than 12 feet. I would select locations naturally moist in preference to land requiring irrigation. A temperature of 60° to 80° in summer, I regard as more favorable than other localities, although they thrive and are profitable in much hotter places."

† "In this part of the State (San Joaquin County), the walnut requires a deep, rich soil, one in which the roots will strike deep, so that there can be no pinch in the hot summer months."

Mr. West has grown the "English" walnut and various French varieties for over twenty years. No irrigation is practiced by him, and unless the walnut finds the conditions mentioned, it is subject to a sudden check of the flow of sap during the summer, which has frequently occurred. The leaves fall and the nuts are left exposed to the hot rays of the sun, and invariably sunburn.

‡ "In planting trees in orchard, first of all plow the ground deep and then go over it with a harrow or pulverizer. Forty feet apart, giving twenty-seven trees to the acre, is the best distance to plant the Improved Soft-Shell walnut. Dig large and deep holes; plant 2 or 3 inches deeper than the trees grew in the nursery; lean them to the prevailing summer winds, and you will not have to stake your trees to make them grow straight. Press the soil firmly around the roots, and if not very moist, give each tree about ten gallons of water, which is sufficient to settle the soil around the roots. Cultivate your orchard to the depth of 5 or 6 inches. If your soil is moist enough to keep the trees in good growing condition during the summer months, irrigation is unnecessary, but to make a first-class walnut, in size and fullness of kernel, if the ground is not naturally moist enough, irrigation will have to be adopted. Small grain should not be planted in a walnut or any other orchard. If corn is grown, leave 8 feet on each side of your trees clear, though I am of the opinion that potatoes, peanuts, or beans are less injurious to the trees."

§ "The usual custom has been, until the last few years, to set two-year-old trees 40 feet apart each way, and plant corn among them as long as it would make a paying crop; experience, however, has demonstrated the fact that it is better to set the trees 50 feet apart each way and reduce the number of rows of corn planted between them each year until it is finally omitted altogether, giving the trees full possession of the soil. This mode of culture usually includes irrigation as long as corn is planted. I think that if the corn and irrigation were left out after the first five years, and the land given clean and thorough cultivation, it would be more profitable for the owners. Shallow cultivation is advocated by the most successful walnut-growers in the valley after the trees have arrived at a bearing age. The old orchards are nearly all planted too close together, and it is reasonable to expect that they will fail to produce good crops sooner than they would if they had been given more room. An examination of any old orchard will show that the outside rows are larger and bear better crops of nuts than the inside ones. Trees twenty years old often have a spread of branches 50 feet across, and I think it safe to say that the roots extend twice as far as the limbs. I have broken roots as large as a pipestem in plowing 25 feet from a tree that has been set seven years. In setting out young trees they should be inclined toward the coast or prevailing winds, and with a little care they can be kept in that position. By using these precautions and insisting on having the tap-root left at least 3 feet long when the trees are

* Hon. Russell Heath, of Carpinteria
† George B. West, of Stockton.
‡ George W. Ford, of Santa Ana.
§ A. Dorman, of Rivera.

dug in the nursery, you will be likely to have your orchard in good shape when it is grown. No limbs should be allowed to grow within at least 6 feet of the ground, as they would interfere with the cultivation of the orchard."

* "The orchard should be thoroughly plowed with a turning plow, early in the spring as soon as the ground is sufficiently dry to work pleasantly. Care should be taken not to plow so deep as to cut the roots, and as the trees are approached the furrows should be shallowed. In some cases fall plowing is practiced, turning the soil from the middle toward the rows and leaving a dead furrow in the middle. In the spring the operation is renewed and the ground left smooth for the summer. This is a good practice on dry land, as it enables the soil to retain a larger part of the winter rainfall. After the spring plowing the land should be thoroughly harrowed and left. Where irrigation is practiced the orchard should be cultivated after each application of water, usually from five to seven times in the season. Where irrigation is not followed the cultivator and weed-cutter should be used as often as necessary, in order to keep down the weeds that would rob the trees of their necessary moisture and plant elements. The great object of cultivation is to keep the surface soil in a loose condition and prevent the evaporation of the moisture required by the trees for their growth. Of course, where inter-tree crops are grown in the orchard, these rules will have to be modified to suit the crops."

† "That the walnut will grow more luxuriantly and bear larger crops at comparatively earlier age in deep and rich bottom land, well drained, well protected, and with plenty of moisture, is an obvious fact; though there arises another question: whether it is advisable to plant walnuts—a class of trees requiring so much space and with so little regard to the nature of the soil—in our richest land so well adapted to the growing of other valuable crops that have *absolutely* to be raised in *rich land*? My experience in walnut culture, and for twenty years I have imported, propagated, and fruited the leading varieties of Europe, besides having collected a large amount of data on that subject from nut-growing countries, warrants me to say that walnut culture can be successfully carried on on the whole Pacific Coast, provided we plant none but *hardy* kinds; in fact, the success of walnut culture in California lies exclusively in the hardiness of the kinds to be planted."

WALNUTS IN OAK LAND.

There has been considerable doubt entertained by growers as to the outcome of walnut orchards planted on oak land. It has been contended that walnut orchards so planted will never be a success; that the roots of the oak remaining in the soil generate poisonous gases, which eventually kill the roots of the walnut with which they come in contact. Various orchards in the vicinity of Santa Barbara are cited as examples.

‡ "The walnut requires well-drained, deep, sandy bottom land, well protected, and where no 'live oak' trees have grown within the last century. Everywhere where the live oak has been recently rooted out, the walnut tree will die about the time it bears the second crop, perhaps earlier. The second planted to replace will die in about the fifth year; the third, in the first, second, or third year. I doubt if any walnut trees will do well where an oak forest has recently existed. The elder Pliny, in his work on Natural History, written nearly two thousand years ago, speaks of this fact existing on the northern coast of the Mediterranean, and cautions planters from attempting fruit-growing where an oak forest has recently existed. There are other causes, no doubt, that will prevent success. Trees will die apparently without cause, and the planter, after waiting ten or a dozen years, will be compelled to root them out and try something else. One half of the orchards that have been planted will never be a success."

§ "I have noticed in the vicinity of Santa Barbara quite a number of 'English' walnuts and other fruit trees being planted on land recently covered by live oak. These orchards can only result in failures, which the owners can ill afford. The precautions laid down in my essay before the Sacramento Convention in 1886 should not be disregarded until it is practically demonstrated that they are without foundation."

¶ "With regard to planting the 'English' walnut on oak land, it is a question that I approach with a great deal of delicacy, especially as I am led to differ from our President (Mr. Cooper), a gentleman whom I esteem as high as any man in the State, as to the poisoning of walnuts. My place of two hundred acres was one mass of oaks, and there is not one single acre of the one hundred and eighty acres now in walnuts but what had

---

* Wm. Moss, of Rivera.
† Mr. Felix Gillet, of Nevada City.
‡ Hon. Ellwood Cooper, essay before State Fruit-Growers' Convention, Sacramento, 1886.
§ Hon. Ellwood Cooper, address before State Fruit-Growers' Convention, Santa Barbara, 1888.
¶ Hon. Russell Heath, address before State Fruit-Growers' Convention, Santa Barbara, 1888.

oaks that would cut from four to fifteen cords of stovewood, and yet I never lost a tree planted among the oaks. Now, whether the oak is poisonous in the soil occupied by Mr. Cooper's orchard and not in Carpinteria, is a question that only the analyzation of the soil can prove; but in my locality the oak is not poisonous to the young walnut. The great mistake, in my opinion, in the raising of the walnut, is that a suitable locality is not obtained.

"Since the above was submitted, I have made thorough examinations of the effects, if any, of the oak on the walnut, and remain of the opinion that the oak does not contain any substance poisonous or detrimental to the walnut. If dead timber is allowed to remain on land, in the decayed trunks may often be found a large worm that feeds on the decayed wood. In my examinations I have never found an instance where these grubs interfere with the living wood of the walnut or any other tree. That many walnuts planted within the last five years have failed to become profitable, and in many instances have died, I think is very easily to be explained.

"The most suitable land for the walnut is the sandy loam; a light, deep, rich soil, with water not nearer the surface than 12 or 15 feet. Many of the planters have disregarded this requirement, and from this cause can be attributed a great proportion of the loss of trees.

"In the Carpinteria Valley the water has been gradually rising. In my orchard in front of my house, where the water was about 18 feet deep when I planted that part of my orchard, it is now less than 6 feet, and I have lost about twenty acres of twenty-five-year-old trees, by the rotting of the roots. I caution all planters to be careful about the depth of water from the surface. In one part of my orchard I had about twenty acres of soft-shell walnuts all in bearing; these trees have died to such an extent that I do not now replace with that variety. I can find no cause for the dying of these trees, and have concluded, with many others in the same fix, that the soft-shell walnut is a short-lived tree."

The writer, in 1886, visited Mr. Cooper's extensive orchards at Ellwood, near Santa Barbara, and he very kindly showed me the walnut orchards where trees had died, and which land was formerly occupied by live oaks. The then existing conditions fully corroborated Mr. Cooper's views, and my observations pointed strongly to two causes: first, oak roots remaining in the soil, which generated poisonous gases that have a deadly effect on other roots; secondly, shallow soil and imperfect drainage, through which causes scores of trees have died all over the State. That poisonous gases are generated by roots of forest trees remaining in the soil, has been fully proven in other parts of the State. As an example, I will cite the orchard of Dr. Edwin Kimball, at Haywards. The land formerly contained many huge sycamore trees; these were dug up and the land planted to prunes, peaches, and apricots. When the apricots attained the bearing age and were in full fruit, they suddenly died down. The exact spot where a sycamore stood is shown by a vacant circle, upon which no tree of original planting stands. Nearly ten years after large roots were unearthed, which still showed life, and upon being exposed emitted a strong, disagreeable, and unbearable odor. There are many other similar cases on record. This same sad experience was met with by other growers, who neglected to extract from the soil the greater portion of the roots, not only of oaks, but also of pines, sycamores, etc. Even willows have been the cause of much trouble. On the other hand, the greater portion of the largest orchards in the State are located where large oaks, pines, and sycamore trees once stood, but care and precision were exercised in removing the roots from the land. There are many who contend that no trees have died in their orchards from this cause, and they ascribe the death of such trees to the time of year the forest trees have been dug up. It is said that if the trees are dug up during the growing period, the roots remaining in the soil will decay in one or two seasons, acting, in this respect, similar to the tree itself when cut back while growing, being full of sap the sudden check causes death; whereas, if dug up in the dormant state, in winter, the roots act as a cutting, keep alive for many

years, and are only prevented from putting forth growth by being under
ground. While the theories advanced are logical, and be the causes
what they may, success can only result where precision is applied. In
places where roots remaining in the ground have caused trouble, the
growers have found that it is best to let the oaks stand, and plant trees,
around them. They are headed back to prevent too much shade, but as
they continue growing the roots do not interfere with the growth of the
orchard trees.

SOIL EXHAUSTION THROUGH THE CULTURE OF THE WALNUT, AND FERTILIZERS TO USE, ETC.

By Prof. S. M. Woodbridge, Ph.D., Agricultural Chemist, Los Angeles. Prepared
by special request.

The walnut crop is involved in more or less mystery, and is little
understood in the abstract, or from a chemical standpoint, although
from a practical standpoint the matter of maintaining the original
integrity of the soil, and in fact the building up of a poor soil, is well
understood and readily accomplished.

To give an illustration, let us look at the orange. In an orchard in
the San Gabriel Valley the soil analyzed 1.14% in potash. Taking the
soil to a depth of only 2 feet, an acre of ground would contain about
100,000 pounds of potash; this potash would be enough to supply an
annual crop of 20,000 pounds of oranges for more than 2,000 years; the
figures from which the above conclusion is drawn are taken from the
report of the State Analyst. Before the orchard was fifteen years old,
it showed marked signs of degeneration. The practical application of
potash in conjunction with nitrates and phosphates, some five years
ago, revived the orchard, and the annual application of a complete
fertilizer has since kept it in a most flourishing condition.

Again, it is a well-known fact that in new ground, suited to the purpose, from 400 to 500 bushels of potatoes can be raised the first year;
the second year scarcely one half that amount can be raised, and the
third year the field would hardly give its seed back; and yet the soil of
such a field would analyze practically the same at the end of the period
as it did at the beginning. Nevertheless, the soil is exhausted from the
practical standpoint of the farmer, that is, he cannot raise a paying
crop of potatoes; and yet from the standpoint of the chemist the soil is
as rich in plant-foods as ever—the little that would have been with-
drawn by three such crops, as are above described, being only the ten
thousandth part of the plant-food in the soil.

What is true in regard to the exhaustion of the soil by an orange or
potato crop is also found to be true in practice in regard to the walnut.

Chemical science has settled the fact that *nitrogen, phosphoric acid,*
and *potash* are the only three expensive elements that any soil is likely
to become deficient in; therefore, as a general rule, those are the only
elements that must be added in order to do everything that is known to
science in order to properly feed any crop. In order, however, to make
these elements, when applied, most effective, the soil must contain a
sufficient amount of humus (decomposing vegetable or animal matter).

It is a well-known fact that the best results are attained in horticulture where circumstances admit of a rotation of crops, the same crop
not being reached oftener than once in four or five years. In an orchard

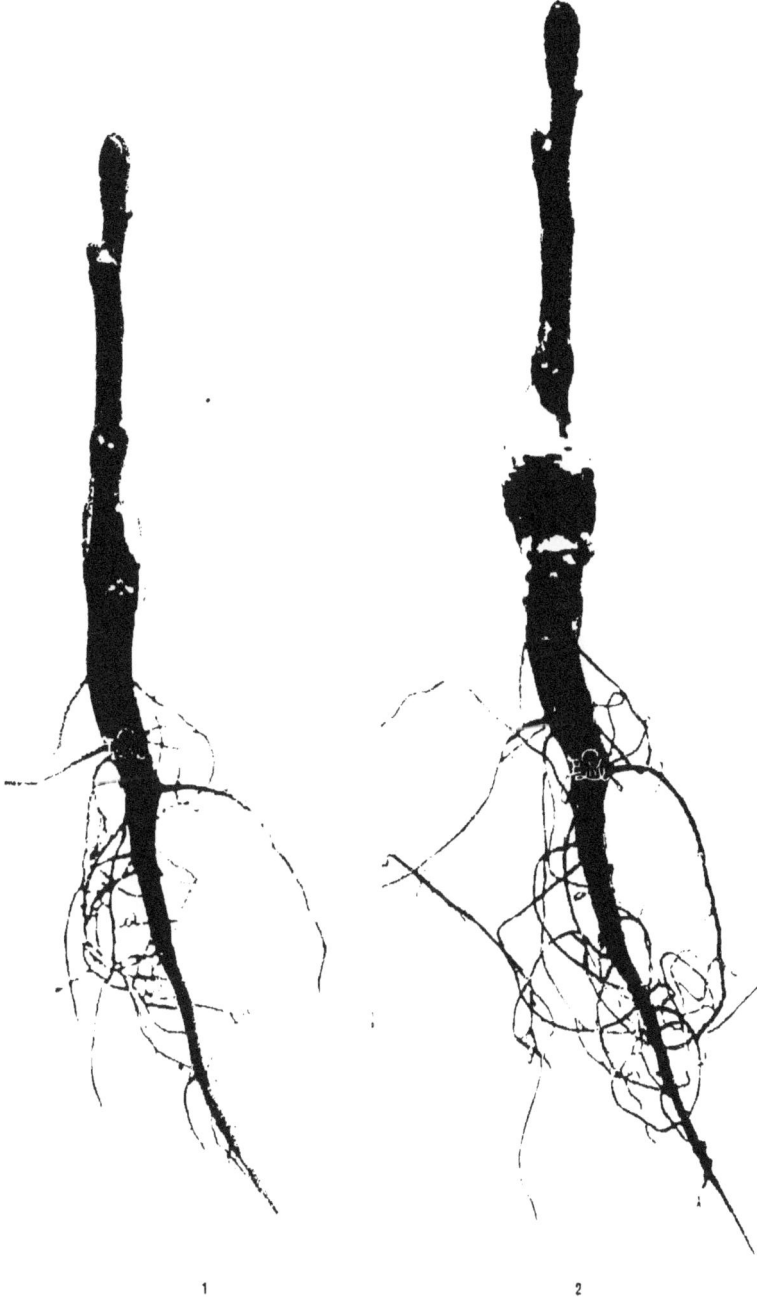

1   2

ROOT-GRAFTING THE WALNUT.

1. Root, with cion inserted, ready for waxing.
2. Root grafted, tied, and waxed over, ready for planting.

it is impossible to rotate a crop, as the trees are set for a lifetime; but the next best thing to a rotation is in keeping up a rotation of green crops for plowing-under, and in this way keep supplying the humus and nitrogen at a nominal cost. These crops, of course, are planted during the fall, and are grown at a time when the tree is dormant.

In order, then, to get the best results from a walnut orchard two things are necessary: (1) Prevent the soil from becoming exhausted; and (2), keep a due amount of humus in the soil.

The first proposition can be done by applying annually these elements in the proportion in which the crop, the wood, and leaf growth may remove them. It would be both amusing and interesting for a rich chemist with little to do and who might own a walnut orchard to ascertain these facts by a collection of all the leaves, new growth, and crop over a series of years, and his report might be most interesting to the few chemists who would read the same, but the farmer could scarcely keep awake over it. What the farmer desires to know is which and how much of the essential elements need to be added, and the cost of such application. To this question the answer can be given by the crop and trees themselves, although the experiments have not been carried over a series of years; but for two succeeding years excellent results have been attained by using to every 4 pounds of nitrogen, 9 pounds of phosphoric acid and 5 pounds of potash in the form of muriate. The phosphoric acid should be in the form of a super-phosphate, that is, treated with *sulfuric* (sulphuric acid), which renders the phosphate readily soluble in water so that it may be immediately available.

A ton of fertilizer containing the fertilizing elements in the above proportions of 4% nitrogen, 9% phosphoric acid, and 5% potash, should not be worth to exceed $35, freight paid.

Now, as to the amounts to be applied: 5 pounds to a tree three years old appears to be the limit from which any good can be derived; 12 pounds per tree to an eight-year-old orchard produces good results, some of the trees yielding 100 pounds and all the trees averaging over 75 pounds of nuts; on eighteen-year-old trees 25 pounds (per tree) was applied with satisfactory results. Taking the case of the eight-year-old trees, the cost of fertilizing an orchard, where the trees were twenty-eight to the acre, would be $5 60, or about 3½% of the value of the crop.

(8) PROPAGATION.

The raising of walnut seedlings is very simple, but great care and attention are required in all points bearing on the germination of the nuts. There are various methods used, but the most simple is as follows: The walnuts are placed in sand, preparatory to planting. A frame, consisting of 12-inch boards set on edge, of any size desired, and resting on the ground, is half-filled with sand; the nuts are then spread thickly (4 to 6 inches) and covered with about 3 or 4 inches of sand. The sand is kept moist, but not too wet, and in case of lack of rain, is watered. An embankment of earth is made all around the frame to prevent the nuts from drying. They are examined from time to time, and as soon as the nuts indicate or show signs of sprouting they are taken up and planted in nursery rows, from 12 to 24 inches apart.

After the first and second years' growth the plants are of a suitable size to bud or graft, or are left in the nursery as seedlings until large enough to transplant into orchard form, the second or third year.

(9) BUDDING THE WALNUT.

There are several methods employed in budding the walnut, among which the following, by the writer (published in 1889*), has proved very successful: Trees are budded in July, August, and as late as September. The bud is cut (shown in Fig. 1) about 1½ inches long. In cutting the bud from the stick the cut is made deep into the wood, the object being to give the bud as much bark as possible. The wood in the bud is then partly removed; it is gouged out with the sharp point

Fig. 1. The bud,
front view.

Fig. 2. The bud, transverse
section.

Fig. 3. The bud,
side view.

of the budding-knife. This is done to allow the inner bark of the bud to unite with the inner bark of the stock, which union would be prevented if the wood in the bud should be allowed to remain. After the wood has been partly removed (as shown in Fig. 2), the bud is inserted into the slit made in the stock, the same as is done in the ordinary method of budding practiced on fruit trees. The bud is then tied tight, with heavy budding twine of at least 18-ply. Three weeks or so afterward, if the bud has "taken," the twine is untied and tied over again; this is done in order to prevent the twine from cutting into the bark. This, however, is not required to be done if the trees are relaxing in growth, or are of such age as to have a bark thick enough to stand the pressure without injury. On young and thrifty growing trees it is best to loosen the twine at the third week, and it should be removed altogether at the fifth or sixth week. The buds are then allowed to lie dormant until spring, when the stocks are cut back to force the bud to start in the month of March or April, according to locality. As the

* Annual Report of State Board of Horticulture, 1889, p. 137.

walnut does not put forth until late in the spring, walnut stocks should not be cut back until they show indications of a rise of sap; with me this has been the most successful time. As soon as the stocks begin to put forth they are cut back and the buds allowed to grow. In cutting back the stocks great care must be exercised. They must not be cut back too close to the bud so as to endanger it, as the stocks invariably have a tendency to die back at the tip, at least an inch or more. As the buds start they are allowed to grow at will until they become hardy; they can then be trained to the remaining portion of the stock or to a stake, in order to produce a straight tree. After the first year's growth they can be transplanted to orchard form.

ANNULAR OR RING BUDDING.

This method is one of the simplest and safest to use on the walnut, and especially adapted to young trees of two or three years old, and to smooth limbs of large trees. In this method a ring is cut right around

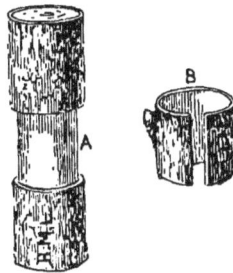

Fig. 4.

A. The stock prepared. *B.* The bud.

the stock, about an inch long. Then a ring of about the same size is taken from the cion, containing a bud, which is slipped into the corresponding space in the stock, and then bound tightly with soft cotton twine or cloth, covering it up to exclude the air. The operation should be performed when the trees are in full growth, during July, August, or September, and left to lie dormant through the winter, to be started in the spring.

(10) GRAFTING THE WALNUT.

Walnut-grafting is not as easily performed as budding. Great care must be exercised in the time and manner in which the operation is performed. The walnut, as a rule, cannot be grafted successfully by the ordinary methods practiced on fruit trees. The reason is that the cions contain but little wood, the pith in them being much greater than in cions of other trees; and when the cion is prepared (wedge-shaped) very little wood is left in it and the bark is so thin that, when inserted, it cannot unite with the stock, not being held firmly in position. Terminal shoots, however, have a thicker bark and more wood and are most successful in grafting. Side grafting is accomplished with success, but can only be performed in the spring, when the sap in the stock begins to rise; this is necessary, as the cion must be inserted when the bark peels, in the same manner as a bud. The walnut does not put forth until quite late in spring, and to secure good, firm wood it becomes necessary to gather the cions before the trees start; and that they may be kept dormant are covered with moist sand and placed in a cellar or cool place. In this way they can be kept until the stocks have made sufficient growth so as to facilitate grafting. I have experimented in grafting the walnut for over twenty years, and the most successful method with me has been the *prong graft* or *prong bud* (of my own origin). (See Plate IX, Figs. 1 to 5, illustrating prong budding.) In this method the small prongs found at the extremity of the shoots are used. (Fig. 2, Plate IX, illustrates the prong—cion—used, and how cut from the branch, reduced one half.) The prong is cut as a *bud*, as shown in the illustration, and the wood is partially removed with the point of a budding-knife, the same as in the method of budding herein described. The stock is first prepared by cutting off with a sharp saw and smoothing over with the knife; a vertical incision is made on the side, and the cion inserted and tied tight with strong budding twine of at least 18-ply. The cuts are waxed over with grafting wax. After the cion has started the graft is examined from time to time, and if it is found that the twine begins to cut into the stock, it is untied and tied again; this will prevent any injury to the stock or cion. The twine, however, should be allowed to remain as long as possible, as it prevents the bark surrounding the slit made on the stock from opening and unseating the cion, which is apt to occur from the action of the atmosphere causing the cion to dry out and die. When the cions have grown from 6 to 12 inches and assumed the functions of the top, this precaution is no longer necessary, and the twine is then removed altogether. The growth of the cions at this time, however, is very tender, and they may be broken off by the slightest touch; as a protection it is well to drive a stake at their side, to which they are tied with some loose material or cloth strips. When this method is employed on large limbs, or on the tops of trees, it is well to tie a piece of limb or wood of any kind on the side of the branch and to which the growth of the cion should be tied. Another good protection is to take a piece of green shoot and tie both ends to the branch so grafted, forming a loop over the bud, to prevent birds, etc., from sitting on the graft and thereby disturbing it.

CLEFT ROOT GRAFTING.

One of the most satisfactory methods practiced on small walnut stocks is the cleft root graft, and its application does not differ materially from the method practiced on pear and apple roots.

The small plants (only one-year-olds are used) are taken up and grafted indoors. (See Plate VII, Figs. 1 and 2.) They are cut off at the crown and split obliquely and the cion (wedge-shape) inserted and immediately tied with 6-ply or 8-ply budding twine or cloth, and waxed.* They are then heeled in sand in some convenient place, exempt from

* Only wax the parts cut or exposed, so that on planting the string or cloth on the parts not waxed may decay and not bind the stock. It is also advisable to cut the twine or cloth on planting.

1.

2   3.

GRAFTING THE WALNUT.

1. The cion prepared.
2. The cion inserted in the stock, ready for waxing.
3. A cion tied and waxed over; growing; three weeks after being grafted in the spring.— From photographs; natural size.

draughts and sunlight, as follows: On the floor of a propagating house or shed moist sand is spread out from 6 to 12 inches deep; then the grafts are put into it standing, thickly, and covered with sand. The entire graft to within an inch or two of the top is covered without injury to it. The sand should always be kept moist, but not too wet, as the bark of the graft is liable to decay; and again, the sand must not be allowed to get dry, as the bark of the graft will shrivel and avoid adhesion. They are kept thus stored from four to six weeks, during which time the parts (cion and stock) callous over; they are then planted in nursery rows, and soon after begin to grow.

TRIANGULAR CROWN GRAFT.

Like the preceding method (cleft root graft) this, too, has proved successful. The stocks (a year old) are not split, but instead a triangular incision is made in the side of the stock, as shown in Fig. 5 at C, about 1 to 1½ inches long. At this point the wood of the stock is generally quite solid and the pith very small. This cut rather consists of taking out of the stock a triangular piece, into which space a cion is inserted of the same shape and size. D shows the space; A the cion prepared for insertion. The cion (from terminal shoots preferred) is prepared to fit the corresponding space, as shown at B, and fitted into the cleft. It is then tied with cloth or twine and waxed over.

This method is also employed with success in the field. The earth is removed from around the stocks and the tree is cut smoothly about the crown or where the swelling of the root begins. The graft being inserted, it is tied with cloth, and waxed. The soil is then banked up against it, covering the graft and stock to within an inch or two of the top of the cion. For making the cleft and facing the cion it is important that the knife be sharp to make a smooth cut. This operation (in the field) is best performed, and most successful, when the stocks begin to show signs of growth late in the spring. The cions are cut late in the fall, or early spring, and kept in sand preparatory to using.

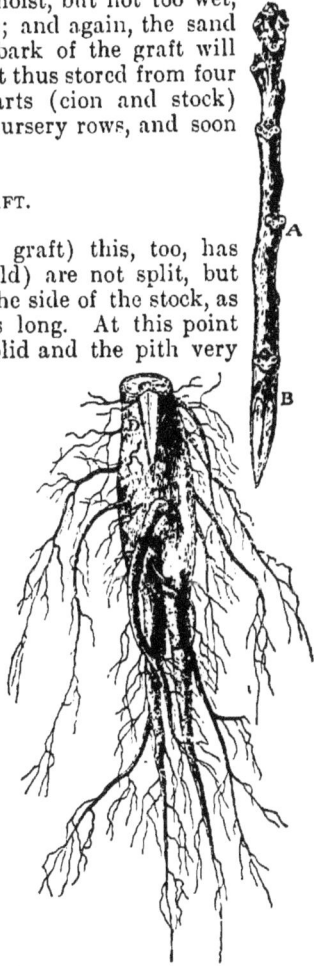

Fig. 5.

CLEFT SAP GRAFT.

Much credit is due to Mr. Felix Gillet, of Nevada City, who has experimented with all sorts of grafting on the walnut for many years, for having given the public the results attained by him in the use of this method. The operation is performed early in the spring when the sap is commencing to flow, and can be used on large limbs from 3 to 5 inches in diameter. The limb is sawed off and smoothed as for ordinary cleft grafting; instead, however, of making a single cleft through the center, two are made, one across the stub at each side of the center, the clefts then being in sapwood instead of through the heartwood and pith. The cion is prepared as for ordinary cleft grafting, for which purpose it is best to use terminal shoots. In cutting the cion great care must be exercised to cut only into the pith of one side. The cion having been inserted, the wound is bound well with cotton cloth and thoroughly waxed.

(11) THE BLACK WALNUT (*Juglans Nigra*, Linn.).

The relative merits of the black walnut for stocks to graft onto have been under consideration for many years, and this root has been extensively tried in this State, with satisfactory results. The variety mostly used is the *Juglans Californica*, or California black walnut. (Plate X, Fig. 11.) In a few instances *Juglans Americana*, or Eastern black walnut (Plate X, Fig. 9), has been tried, but preference was given to the former, being indigenous to our State. The Japanese walnut (*Juglans Sieboldiana*) has also been tried, and has proved quite satisfactory, but is not as strong a grower as the *Californica*. For a time I was loath to believe the stock would influence the graft and cause it to produce nuts of a dark shell. Experiments, however, have proved the contrary. Trees now in bearing for over twenty years show no variation in color of shell, but an improvement in kernel and quality of the nuts. The stocks are thrifty and healthy, easy of propagation, and easily budded and grafted. Some twenty years ago I commenced experimenting in grafting and budding the wild walnut, with very satisfactory results. A plot of *Juglans rupestris*, growing along the mountains in Los Angeles County, was worked over to different varieties very satisfactorily, but the stock is quite scrubby and of such dwarf habit that it can only be recommended for dwarf purposes. The grafts took well and made splendid growth. In all tests made on trees in the wild state, nuts were produced on buds and grafts the second and third years. In some cases the nuts were quite small, due perhaps to the stunted condition of the stocks, for all must have been very old. The buds and grafts that made the strongest growth were on stocks which did not look so aged. These are now producing fine nuts, equal to those from the parent tree.

The oldest walnut orchard budded on the *Californica* is at Winters, Yolo County, and the trees are over twenty years old. This orchard has produced fine crops yearly and the nuts show a marked improvement over those produced by the parent trees.

At Vacaville two rows of large black walnut trees (*J. Californica*) were worked over to different varieties of the "English" or "Persian" walnut very successfully, by the prong bud method, described elsewhere, and the ordinary cleft sap graft. The trees were planted some thirty years ago for shade along the roadside. In the winter of 1892 the limbs were cut back to the crotch or main stem. In the spring they put forth numerous shoots, which were thinned out to a dozen or so to each tree, according to the spread of the branches. These new shoots were budded in the summer. Those that did not "take" were grafted in the winter. Thus a fine stand of buds and grafts was obtained, which commenced to bear the second and third years. They now form large spreading heads, and bear regularly.

The process of converting these apparently worthless trees, except for shade, into fruitful trees, was very simple, and has proved remunerative and entirely satisfactory to its projector.

In Ventura County are to be seen many walnut orchards of recent planting budded and grafted on this stock. This was brought about by the satisfactory results obtained from walnut orchards so worked of early planting. In the past few years large plantings of walnuts have been made, and many growers have given preference to trees grafted and budded on this stock—*J. Californica.*

VARIETIES OF THE BLACK WALNUT.

Since the relative merits of stocks for the walnut have been discussed, it is deemed proper to append a list of varieties with which further trials can be made. The following varieties and their description (marked with *) are taken from a bulletin on "Nut Culture in the United States," issued by the Division of Pomology of the Department of Agriculture:

Gordon.—"Size large, form cubical, slightly conical at each end, shell of medium thickness, cracking qualities good, kernel light-colored, plump, quality excellent."—Virginia.

Missouri.—"Size medium, form oval, compressed, with quite smooth shell, cracking qualities good, kernel light-colored, plump, flavor pleasant, quite free from the grossness characterizing the species; quality very good."—Missouri.

Peanut.—"A rather small pyriform nut. The shell is thin and easily cracked, while the kernel, which is in the larger end of the nut, comes out entire. The kernel is white and of delicate flavor."—Ohio.

Nurza.—"A large nut with thin shell, kernel large and of good flavor. Also a strong grower."—Ohio.

Taylor.—"A quadrangular-pointed nut of good size. The shell is thin and easily broken with a slight blow. The kernel is large, coming out in halves; the meat is white and of fine quality."—Ohio.

Thomas.—"Size large, form oblate, compressed, slightly pointed at base, considerably so at apex, shell medium to thin, cracking qualities medium, the kernel not easily removed in perfect halves from the shell, flavor sweet, rich, quality good to very good."—Pennsylvania.

American ("*Eastern*") (Plate X, Fig. 9).—So called by reason of having been produced from seed imported from the East. The tree is large and handsome, and reproduces itself or "comes the same" from seed. The seed germinates easily, and the plants stand transplanting and are easily budded and grafted. It makes a beautiful shade tree along driveways and avenues. The nut is of medium size, very dark, and somewhat furrowed, and hard.

California (*Juglans Californica,* Watson) (Plate X, Fig. 11).—A rapid-growing tree, indigenous to the central and northern parts of the State. It occurs nowhere below the Sierra Madre Mountains and Coast Range in the wild state. "Comes the same" from seed, stands transplanting, and is easily budded and grafted. The nut is of medium size, shell quite hard, and smooth. The kernel is quite rich and oily. This stock has come into great favor for budding and grafting onto. The tree attains great height, and many trees are to be seen over 100 feet high, and of great dimensions. This species has been confounded with the Dwarf or Wild Walnut (*J. rupestris*) indigenous to the southern part of the State, extending from the Tehachapi Mountains into Arizona and Mexico.

Dwarf or *Wild Walnut* (*Juglans rupestris*, Eng.).—This species is indigenous to the southern part of the State, extending from the Tehachapi Mountains to the south. It is a small, dwarfish tree, but a vigorous grower. "Comes the same" from seed, and is easily budded and grafted, also bears transplanting. The nut is quite small, very hard and smooth, but of little or no commercial value.

(12) PRUNING THE WALNUT.

* "During the first year constant pruning is necessary to have the tree properly shaped. I have pruned in a summer as many as four or five times. Branches are apt to grow too rapidly, bear down with their own weight, and break off during high winds, destroying the symmetry of the tree and occasioning much loss of time. All lateral branches growing from the leader should be cultivated to assume an upward angle of about 15° to 45° from the main leader. This can be done by clipping off all branches growing under, and at times cutting off the ends. A trunk should be maintained free from limbs 3½ to 4½ feet from the ground. Earth should be kept away from the trunks, and if the top roots near the trunk are exposed, so much the better; it will assist the tree in breathing. The most careful cultivation is necessary, and nothing, after the fifth year, should be grown between the rows, unless you have plenty of water to irrigate by flooding all the ground once every eight weeks; if you are so prepared, sow your orchard in alfalfa, and do no cultivating."

† "Pruning the walnut is extremely simple and can be done by any one. When planting the tree, don't cut the top off of one-year-old trees, but it is absolutely necessary to cut back a two or a three-year-old tree; in fact, the finest young walnut orchard I know of in Orange County (and we have lots of fine ones down this way) was grown from two-year-old trees from 8 to 10 feet high, and cut back to about 4½ feet, and all limbs below that trimmed off, except three or four, which were allowed to grow up and make the top of the tree   Never prune the trees over 3½ feet, as the bark of a tree is easily sunburned, and thus it is necessary for the foliage to shade the trunk. If the lower limbs extend outward and are in the way of the cultivator, tie them up, for by so doing you can train the lower branches upward, so as to cultivate close to the tree, and when the orchard comes into bearing the limbs growing upward will not bend down to the ground with the fruit, so you cannot get within twenty feet of them with the cultivator."

‡ "In pruning it has been the custom to trim to a height of 6 to 7 feet, but I think 4 to 5 feet better. Such high pruning makes the tree top-heavy, and the prevailing winds cause them to lean, exposing one side of the trunk to the sun, thus causing sunburn. I think it best to trim little, if any. It is the nature of the tree to allow the limbs to grow downward and fill any space of account that may have been made by pruning, while if allowed to grow in their natural state, the limbs will start near the ground, growing upward and keeping out of the way much better than when allowed to hang down. I have not been able as yet to grow them just as I would like in this respect, on account of raising crops (mostly corn) between the trees, and I find it very difficult to save the lower limbs while young and tender, as a very little push or strain when plowing will injure them next to the trunk, and they should then be cut off to save the tree from greater injury than the loss of a limb. Avoid crotches or forks. If a tree is about evenly divided the abundance of foliage the tree has in summer will cause it to split with a very little wind, and you will thus lose the use of the tree for several years, if not altogether. If badly broken, start a new shoot near the ground, and in six years, with care, it will be a bearing tree."

* Hon. Ellwood Cooper, Santa Barbara.
† George W. Ford, Santa Ana.
‡ C. A. Caufman, of Rivera, in "California Cultivator and Poultry Keeper," October, 1896.

1. Prong-bud growing, showing the stock where first cut back and waxed over; also the twine tied loosely to prevent the opening of the bark and endangering the bud.
2. The bud prepared, ready for insertion into the slit in the stock.
3. The stock prepared, ready to receive the bud.
4. The bud inserted, before being tied.
5. The operation complete.—From photographs; natural size.

(13) HARVESTING.

Harvesting the walnut is very simple, as most of the nuts do not have to be picked, for they, of their own accord, drop to the ground at maturity; yet considerable attention must be paid to the gathering of the crops so as to have clean, bright nuts that may command a high price and ready sale. The walnut harvest begins in September and ends in November. In some sections the crop comes in quite early and is gathered in September, overlapping into October; in others, the crop is not harvested so early; but October is the principal month, sometimes overlapping into November.

Some of the growers collect the nuts from the ground as they fall every day, others collect them every other day, and some every third day, until most of the crop has fallen of its own accord, and those remaining on the trees are knocked down by means of a pole. Boys and men are also employed to climb the trees and shake the nuts down; others agitate the limbs with a long pole having a hook at the end. The nuts that are ready to drop come down easily, and are picked up and dried on trays in the sun. It generally takes from three to four pickings to gather all the nuts from a tree. When the husk inclosing the nut shows no signs of cracking it is an indication that the nut is yet unripe, and when knocked down the kernels of many of these generally dry away and do not fill well. Then, again, if the nuts are allowed to hang on the trees or remain on the ground too long after falling, they absorb moisture and rapidly deteriorate in flavor, color, and keeping qualities. In the walnut sections along the coast damp fogs and dew prevail during the harvest time, rendering the husks quite moist, and the nuts contained inside become stained by the acid juice of the husks, which, if not removed, renders the nuts quite black, and lessens their market value. This acid is very strong and adhesive, and to remove it the nuts have to be washed and afterward dried. Hon. Ellwood Cooper, of Santa Barbara, has a most perfect apparatus for washing and drying the walnut, which is an invention of his own. It consists of an iron cylinder with a long opening on the top side, where the nuts are put in. When the nuts are washed the cylinder will turn with the opening down, thus letting the walnuts and water out. As with all other apparatus of this kind, it has to be seen to be appreciated. They are made by the Fulton Iron Works, of San Francisco, and cost from $125 to $140.

* "The 'hard' shells should and the 'soft' and 'paper' shells *must* be gathered as soon as possible after dropping from the trees, as it injures the quality and appearance of the nuts to remain long on the ground. They are usually dried on trays about 3 feet wide by 6 feet long, holding about one hundred pounds each. 'Soft' and 'paper' shells should be dried in the shade, and many of the growers have buildings for that purpose. After they are thoroughly dried they are bleached and then run over a screen with a one-inch mesh, into strong sacks of uniform size, each sack bearing the registered trade-mark of the 'Los Nietos and Ranchito Walnut Growers' Association,' and also the name of the individual grower, thereby settling the question of responsibility in case the nuts are not up to the required standard."

† "There are different modes of gathering: some clean the trees at once, and others go over them several times. I pick what has fallen without knocking. I then tap those limbs lightly on which the nuts are ripest, and the third time over I aim to clean the trees. The walnuts are picked up and put in sacks and barrels, so as to be easily

* A. Downer, of Rivera.
† Joseph Sexton, essay before Ninth State Fruit-Growers' Convention, 1888.

3—W

handled, and hauled to a sunny place to dry, and should be placed on elevated platforms made of narrow boards, with spaces of one fourth of an inch between each board. The platform should be about 8 feet wide and 40 feet long, or as long as two men can handle a canvas to cover the beds, which should be done every night the dew falls. The nuts should be stirred in these beds once or twice each day, and with favorable weather they will dry sufficiently in three days, and are ready for market. I have always dried my walnuts by the sun and they have given good satisfaction, and for small orchards I think it is the cheapest and best way. Some dry by evaporation and claim it is preferable to the sun; that it sets the oil quickly and prevents the nut from becoming rancid. Others claim that it makes them so; but be this as it may, those having large orchards cannot depend on drying all by natural heat, and the drier will have to be used, even if it is not so good for the nut."

*"In handling the nuts, I cure in dry-houses by artificial heat, heating sufficient to evaporate the water and set the oil of the nut. When this is done the nuts will keep sweet for an indefinite time. I have kept them as an experiment, in my store-house, which is of concrete, for five years, and at the end of that time they were as sweet as when first cured. With my facilities, I cure them in eight hours. In preparing them for market, I have a washing apparatus—invented by Mr. Cooper—which I use if the nuts are discolored, as they often are by coming in contact with leaves or shucks when there is dew or rain. Directly after washing they are thoroughly dried and cured in the dry-house."

†"In gathering soft-shells, the nuts should not be left long on the ground, as the sun and fog will cause the shell to crack and the nut to become ruined. They should not be left long in the gathering-sacks, as they will then sweat and turn black. If the nuts are to be washed it should be done as soon as emptied from the picking-sacks, as they will then clean much easier. After this, spread in trays for drying. If to be bleached they should be thoroughly dry before. We use trays 3 by 6 feet, with sides 4 or 6 inches high, and a slat bottom with ¼-inch space between slats. For the past few years all walnuts grown in Rivera have been scoured by placing them in a wire cylinder, washing them and revolving it for five or ten minutes, or longer if necessary to make them clean, then throw on water enough to wash clean before taking out of washer. This greatly improves their appearance, removing all fiber and pieces of hull that might be sticking to them. It also gives them a much smoother appearance. Now place them in trays, and dry."

ANNUAL AND BIENNIAL CROPS.

During many years the opinion entertained by many, that the walnut was a biennial bearer—that is, a crop could only be expected every other year—became prevalent, and was generally believed. This idea originated in the minds of some who could not be satisfied unless they saw *all trees* heavily laden with walnuts every year, and also owing to many of the orchards being planted to those singular and unproductive trees referred to elsewhere. On this account—the idea having become general—many hesitated about going into the business. As a rule, fruit-growers are not accustomed to wait for results, as one must do in the case of the walnut. Since the principal walnut plantations have come into bearing, this idea has been dispelled, it having been proved a fallacy. For about twelve years the orchards of twenty years ago have been bearing, and while they prove to be regular bearers, show that one year they bear a heavy crop, and the next one not so heavy, but a *crop* may be depended on every year; so that the walnut, while it may be considered a biennial bearer, must be classed as a tree producing regular crops, or a good bearer.

COMMERCIAL GRADES.

The walnut crop of the State is classified commercially under the following category, viz.:

Hard-shells include all nuts having a hard shell; these take in the numerous varieties of the so-called "English" walnut.

* Hon. Russell Heath, essay before Eleventh State Fruit-Growers' Convention, 1889.
† C. A. Caufman, of Rivera, in "California Cultivator and Poultry Keeper," October, 1896.

Soft-shells include all nuts having a soft shell, and take in the improved varieties of the so-called "English" walnut, and foreign varieties of this texture.

Paper-shells include varieties of walnuts having an extra thin shell. The walnut-growers of Southern California have agreed upon a uniform method of grading, which is by passing the nuts over a screen with a one-inch mesh, and making two grades only for the market. The paper-shells are kept separate, and sold as a fancy grade. The marketing methods adopted by the coöperative societies are to receive the nuts from the growers as they come from the orchard, and sulphur, grade, sack, and sell them.

The walnut is marketed in sacks, specially made, and holding about 120 pounds. Some, however, use the common grain sack, holding about 65 pounds. Before sacking, many growers place the walnuts in a wire cylinder of one-inch mesh, the friction of which on revolving gives the nuts a smooth appearance, and thus adds to their commercial value.

(14) ENEMIES OF THE WALNUT.

The walnut, so far, has fewer enemies than most trees, and the few that attack it are not considered detrimental to its culture in a high degree, for they are easily subdued. These are treated of separately in this chapter.

RED SPIDER.

Tetranychus telarius.

This spider, or mite, attacks different species of trees, shrubs, etc., also the walnut. It is very small, and can hardly be seen without the aid of a glass.

This insect, while not very troublesome on the walnut, is kept in check by dusting sulphur over the trees. The lime, sulphur, and salt solution, applied in winter, and the summer remedy, given below, have practically exterminated the pest on walnut trees.

Winter Remedy.—Unslacked lime, 40 pounds; sulphur, 20 pounds; stock salt, 15 pounds; water to make 60 gallons. Place 10 pounds of lime and 20 pounds of sulphur in a boiler, with 20 gallons of water, and boil over a brisk fire, for not less than one hour and a half, or until the sulphur is thoroughly dissolved. When this takes place, the mixture will be of an amber color. Next place in a cask 30 pounds of unslacked lime, pouring over it enough hot water to thoroughly slack it; and, while it is boiling, add the 15 pounds of salt. When this is dissolved, add to the lime and sulphur in the boiler, and cook for half an hour longer, when the necessary amount of water to make the 60 gallons should be added.

Summer Remedy.—Sulphur, 3 pounds; caustic soda (98%), 2 pounds; whale-oil soap, 25 pounds; water to make 100 gallons. Boil the sulphur and caustic soda together in about 2 gallons of water; when the sulphur becomes dissolved, add the soap and boil until thoroughly dissolved, then add water to make 100 gallons of solution, and apply warm.

YELLOW SPIDER OR MITE.

Tetranychus.

Apply same treatment as for red spider.

WALNUT SCALE.

Aspidiotus Juglans regia, Coms.

The walnut is subject to infection from this scale peculiar to itself, and known as the walnut scale. The scale, however, has not proved a pest among our walnut trees. The old trees do not suffer from its attacks, as it infests the large limbs principally.

Remedy (applied when trees are dormant in winter).—Lime, 25 pounds; sulphur, 20 pounds; salt, 15 pounds. Take 10 pounds of lime, 20 pounds of sulphur, and 20 gallons of water; boil until the sulphur is thoroughly dissolved. Take the remaining 15 pounds of lime and 15 pounds of salt, and when thoroughly slacked, mix together and add enough water to make in all 60 gallons of solution; strain and spray warm.

BROAD-NECK BORER.

Prionus lacticollis, Drury.

This gigantic beetle appears during July and August, but at times much earlier, and also late in winter. The beetle measures from 1¼ to

Fig. 6.

2 inches in length. Color dark brown, nearly black. Possesses strong, thick jaws. In the male the antennæ are rather slender; in the female they are not so stout, and the body is much broader. The larva (Fig. 7) is a large borer with a broad neck. It measures from 2½ to 3 inches in length. The color of the larva is yellowish white. The head is quite small and is reddish brown. There is a light blue line down the back. As a rule it mostly attacks trees and vines just below the surface. It bores a hole through the center of the root, or into the trunk. On the trunk of trees and vines it never bores very deep, seemingly preferring

to work just under the bark. The larva cannot easily be discovered, for the reason that the trees do not begin to show the effects until the larva has had time to develop to its full size, when it becomes a voracious feeder. The larva remains in that state three days, and changes to the chrysalis state about the month of June, as the beetles generally make their appearance in July.

Remedy.—It is very difficult to ascertain the presence of borers before the trees indicate their presence. Walnut trees sometimes are observed to be bleeding (oozing sap) from a certain spot; this indicates a borer, or having been damaged otherwise. However, the cause should be

Fig. 7.

carefully looked into by cutting into the bark, and the borer destroyed. The wound should then be covered over with such material that will prevent the action of the atmosphere from injuring the tree.

SPAN WORM.

In 1891 there appeared in this State, at Santa Barbara, a caterpillar commonly known as the "span worm," infesting the walnut in great numbers, and in some places the trees were almost completely defoliated. The insect is easily subdued by the following remedy: Paris green, 1 pound; water, 200 gallons. The remedy is applied as soon as the caterpillars make their appearance in the spring.

WALNUT APHIS.

This insect attacks the walnut in some sections, and its exudations form on the tree a sort of "honey dew," which forms into a fungus and renders the foliage and husks quite black.

The black Australian ladybugs, *Rhizobius ventralis*, *Rhizobius debclis*, and *Rhizobius Toowoombæ*, have kept this insect in check, through which agencies the injury is not felt.

WALNUT BACTERIOSIS.

The only known disease, aside from "root knot," reported as attacking the walnut, which has caused some alarm, is a species of fungi.

*"It is not known as yet whether the primary cause of the trouble is due to some derangement of the vital functions of the plant or to parasitic organisms. The progress and destructive action of the disease are certainly very apparent. A small black spot first appears on the side of the nut husk while the kernel is still in the milk. The death of tissue beneath this spot gradually extends, spreading inward, and soon reaches the shell. Unless the shell is already hard the decay penetrates through the soft meat of the nut within, and the whole is soon disorganized and turns black. * * * A study

*Report of Division of Vegetable Pathology, Department of Agriculture, 1893, p. 272.

of the diseased tissue shows the presence of a bacillus, the organism being constantly present. Pure cultures of the bacillus have been obtained from spring inoculations, the tissue of the nut husk being too firm in the latter part of the season to test the action of the organism with any degree of certainty. Observations indicate that unfavorable root conditions for the trees may have an important bearing on the primary development of the trouble."

This disease was reported as being prevalent among walnut trees in the central part of the State in 1891. Since then, however, the trees are said to have recovered, and, on investigation, it was found that it was not this disease, but the trouble was caused by the soil drying out in the summer, causing the trees to lose considerable of their foliage and the nuts to shrivel.

This bacterial or mysterious disease has made its appearance in various walnut orchards in different parts of the State, and threatens to seriously affect the walnut groves unless checked by some effective remedy. The disease has been termed *Bacteriosis* of walnuts, by Prof. Newton B. Pierce, Assistant U. S. Pathologist, and is described* by him as follows:

"Bacteriosis of walnuts is a bacterial disease of the nut, branch, and leaf parts of the Persian walnut (*Juglans regia*). Inoculation experiments have demonstrated that other forms of *Juglans* may also be artificially infected by the organism. Under natural conditions the nut of the Persian tree is very commonly infected in the blossom, at or about the time of pollination. Secondary infections may take place through any portion of the hull of the tender nut, especially during the more rapid growth of spring. The new shoots and leaves may be infected at any portion which is tender and rapidly growing, but most of these infections actually take place at or near the growing point of such shoots, and only become distinct to the naked eye after rapid growth has left the infected part some distance down the branch. Injury to the cells of the nut, branch, or leaf parts is effected by the organism by means of an enzym, or ferment. This enzym acts chemically upon the tissues surrounding the point of infection, destroying the cells and preparing them as pabulum for the multiplying bacilli. This enzym is capable of destroying the tender cells of the hull, newly forming shell, and the contents of the kernel. As any or all of these parts become hard with age, less injury is done through infection by this germ. In case of blossom infection the nut is usually badly diseased, and, in a majority of cases, will fall when one third or two thirds grown. Lateral infection of the hull is less likely to wholly destroy the nut, but very commonly causes it to fall or the hull to adhere to the shell in such a manner as to make the nut unfit for market. Wherever the nut becomes infected the parts eventually turn back, owing to the oxidation of the tannic acid. When the disease is actually spreading, however, a circle next the healthy tissue usually assumes a watery appearance, which may be used as a character quite distinctive of this disease. This watery ring is where the enzym is acting upon the healthy cells often in advance of the presence of the organism itself. The characters here given for infected nuts are equally applicable to infected branches.

"The germs of this disease are capable of wintering either in the diseased branch or nut.

"The treatment of walnut bacteriosis has already shown some beneficial results. Over forty acres of spraying experiments were set on foot last spring. This work was done with the leading fungicides, but as the disease is now known to be of bacterial nature, it will be attempted to prevent the same by means of some of the leading germicides, with which, applied as winter sprays, it is hoped to obtain even better and cheaper results than with the standard fungicides. As this work is still in progress, and certainly cannot be completed inside of another year, it cannot be summarized at this time. It may be said, however, in absence of the perfection of better methods, that the Bordeaux mixture applied to the tree just before the growth of spring starts, and again to the nuts as soon after pollination as possible, will certainly prevent a portion of the infections which would otherwise take place. It has also been found of advantage to gather and destroy diseased nuts, and to prune away diseased branches during the winter. It is hoped that another season given to the testing of germicides may develop some more specific manner of preventing infection. No treatment looking to the cure of diseased nuts or branches may be hoped for; all treatment must be preventive."

In the "California Fruit-Grower" of October 17, 1896, Professor Pierce adds to the above the following note:

"The walnut disease has a wide distribution on this coast, extending as far north as Stockton, and south to San Diego County. There probably are, however, large intervening regions not affected. The disease does no special damage to the year-old wood

* In California Fruit-Grower, September 26, 1896.

only spreading a new growth, hence there is no danger whatever of the tree being killed outright—it is largely a matter of loss of crop and injury to spring growth. Its spread will largely depend on the atmospheric conditions each spring. Moisture of the atmosphere is favorable to the disease, and a dry atmosphere is unfavorable to it."

ROOT KNOT OR GALLS.

(Plate XVII, Fig. 2.)

Among walnut trees these so-called "root knots" or "galls" have of late been quite prevalent. The origin of this curious disease is not fully known, but, in some cases, it is the work of a minute insect—the nematode. So far, the best remedy is to cut away the knots or galls and completely remove the affected wood, and apply a solution of bluestone in the fall, as strong as the water will dissolve. This is applied with a swab, and the earth again thrown back. The safest way to use bluestone is in the form of *Bordeaux* mixture, which can be applied any time of year. Take sulphate of copper, 16 pounds; lime, 30 pounds. Dissolve the sulphate of copper in 22 gallons of water; in another vessel slack the lime in 6 gallons of water. When the latter mixture has cooled, pour it slowly into the copper solution, care being taken to mix the fluids by constant stirring.

(15) AREA OF WALNUT CULTURE IN STATE.

The walnut is now found growing throughout the State in almost every county. In 1892 a tree census was made by the State Board of Horticulture, through agents in the field, and the following acreage was found to be in walnuts:

County.	Bearing, Acres.	Not Bearing, Acres.	Total Acres.
Alameda	28	8	36
Alpine			
Amador	3	6	9
Butte	5	7	12
Calaveras	12	11	23
Colusa	20	40	60
Contra Costa		50	50
Del Norte			
El Dorado	3	5	8
Fresno*	10	60	70
Glenn	30	50	80
Humboldt	3		3
Inyo	1	3	4
Kern	30	41	71
Kings			
Lake	15	60	75
Lassen		2	2
Los Angeles	1,752	37	1,789
Marin		1	1
Mariposa	8	4	12
Mendocino			
Merced	7	7	14
Modoc			
Mono			
Monterey	7	16	23
Napa	12	28	40
Nevada	13	6	19
Orange	1,467	1,125	2,592

* Before Madera County was formed.

AREA OF WALNUT CULTURE IN STATE—Continued.

County.	Bearing, Acres.	Not Bearing, Acres.	Total Acres.
Placer	7	15	22
Plumas			
Sacramento	26	18	44
San Benito	35	9	44
San Bernardino*	131	70	201
San Diego	389	178	567
San Joaquin	27	42	69
San Luis Obispo	245	234	479
San Mateo			
Santa Barbara	1,117	786	1,903
Santa Clara	10	7	17
Santa Cruz	3	10	13
Shasta			
Sierra	2		2
Siskiyou	1	1	2
Solano	12	57	69
Sonoma	38	42	80
Stanislaus		3	3
Sutter	13	2	15
Tehama	4	26	30
Trinity	20		20
Tulare	4	8	12
Tuolumne	7	6	13
Ventura	997	5,308	6,305
Yolo			
Yuba	5	3	8
Totals	6,520	8,392	14,912

No reports were made from Alpine, Del Norte, Modoc, Mono, and Plumas counties, where it is doubtful, on account of climatic conditions, if walnut trees will grow. On the other hand, no reports were received from Mendocino, San Mateo, Shasta, and Yolo counties, where orchards of recent planting are located. Thus it will be seen that the bulk of the walnut orchards are in the lower counties, where the tree finds a congenial home and most favorable conditions essentially required. Ventura County leads, with 6,305 acres; Orange is next, with 2,592 acres; Santa Barbara is third, with 1,903 acres; then comes Los Angeles with 1,789 acres, San Diego with 567 acres, San Luis Obispo with 479 acres, and San Bernardino with 201 acres. The total acreage in the State in that year was given at 14,912 acres, of which 6,520 were in bearing. Readers no doubt understand how difficult it is to obtain accurate statistics, and while we make no pretention of the above figures being strictly correct, yet we believe they are approximately correct and show to what extent this industry is carried on in the various counties. The County Assessors are obliged to gather a complete tree census every year, and while they endeavor to comply with the law as well as they can, they are hindered from furnishing a true account through the laxity of the growers, who reluctantly give the figures of their orchards. The gathering of such statistics yearly, however, serves a good purpose, as the reports show where fruits of the different kinds are produced and the extensions that are made in this line.

* Before Riverside County was formed.

According to the Assessors' returns there were growing in 1896 the following number of walnut trees in the State, in the various counties:

Alameda	2,200	Marin	75	Sacramento	3,272	Sierra	50
Amador	250	Mariposa	280	San Benito	3,405	Solano	2,979
Butte	1,185	Madera	71	S'n Bernardi'o	11,500	Sonoma	4,286
Calaveras	500	Mendocino	112	San Diego	19,491	Stanislaus	270
Colusa	7,880	Merced	933	San Joaquin	2,475	Sutter	2,734
Contra Costa	4,650	Modoc	56	S'n L'is Obispo	17,595	Tehama	7,414
El Dorado	1,125	Monterey	478	San Mateo	400	Trinity	50
Fresno	2,279	Napa	11,350	Santa Barbara	21,010	Tulare	350
Glenn	12,000	Nevada	3,000	Santa Clara	11,601	Tuolumne	985
Inyo	390	Orange	137,223	Santa Cruz	4,580	Ventura	69,819
Kern	981	Placer	1,685	Shasta	2,406	Yuba	1,900
Los Angeles	140,675	Riverside	7,803				

Total _____ _____ _____ 525,753

NOTE.—The Assessor of Lake County returns the following figures, which are not in the above list, viz.: Under one year, 10,083; under two years, 351; under three years, 32; under four years, 308.

The walnut is generally planted at from 40 to 50 feet apart, and as an average 40 feet would be safe to calculate the acreage of the State. Therefore, allowing twenty-seven trees to the acre, at 40 feet apart, we have in the State 19,472 acres in 1896, as per Assessors' returns, of which 8,814 acres are in bearing, and 10,658 acres are non-bearing.

VALUATION OF WALNUT ORCHARDS.

As indicating the value of a walnut orchard (irrespective of the land or location), the following schedule of valuations, fixed by a convention of Assessors of the southern counties in 1891, is appended:

1 to 3 years planted	$5 00 per acre.
4 years planted	10 00 per acre.
5 years planted	15 00 per acre.
6 years planted	20 00 per acre.
15 years planted	100 00 per acre.

(15) CULTURAL RANGE OF THE WALNUT (*Juglans Regia*) IN THE UNITED STATES.

According to "Nut Culture in the United States," the cultural range of the walnut in the United States is mostly confined to the Pacific Coast, and California in particular. *"East of the Rocky Mountains the Persian walnut has been most successful in a limited area along the Atlantic slope, from New York southward through New Jersey, southwestern Pennsylvaia, central Virginia, North Carolina, and Georgia. The tree endures the winters in favored localities near the coast as far north as Connecticut, Rhode Island, and Massachusetts, but has never been planted there except in very small way. Some very fine old trees are reported from Rochester, N. Y., where they are in old gardens in the suburbs of the city. The finest and most fruitful specimens reported are at Fordham, N. Y., Princeton, N. J., Germantown and Philadelphia, Pa., and Georgetown, D. C., some of these being a hundred years old and bearing large crops of nuts of fair quality."

*"Nut Culture in the United States." Special Report, Department of Agriculture, 1896, p. 29.

A few trees are mentioned as existing at Marietta, Pa., at Red Hill, Va., at Fall Church, Va., in Delaware, Florida, and the Mississippi Valley, with fair and no success. In Michigan but few trees have been planted, and late experiments in a limited way in Indiana are quite promising, also in Kentucky and Tennessee. In Louisiana a few experiments promise well, but are very limited in scope, and the same is said of Texas. In Arizona the walnut has been planted quite extensively, and from specimens exhibited from there, that territory is bound to become a competitor with California in the walnut trade, and the same applies to Oregon, where the industry is now being pursued. In California the walnut finds the conditions for its culture the most favorable, and the industry is extending annually.

(17) WALNUT-GROWING IN EUROPE.*

By Hon. Eugene Germain, U. S. Consul, Zurich, Switzerland.

In answer to a letter from the Los Nietos and Ranchito Walnut-Growers' Association of California, of June 4th, requesting information about the foreign walnut crop, I said:

."Switzerland does not grow walnuts on a large scale, but almost every farmer in the valleys has a few trees scattered on his ranch, and principally along the roadways. The annual output is small and some years not sufficient to supply the home demand. In years of abundance, a good article of salad oil is made from walnuts. The trees are hardy and not subject to scale, blight, or other diseases, the only serious enemy of the walnut being late frosts, of which there were none this season. The principal walnut-growing districts of Europe are France, Italy, and Austria-Hungary.

"I will at once take the necessary steps to obtain the information you desire, and within two weeks or so post you, if possible, on this season's crop outlook."

I now beg to inform the association, through the Department, that from reports I have received from the United States Consuls at Frankfort, Vienna, Naples, Bordeaux, Marseilles, Castellamare, and Sorrento, I am able to report as follows:

Walnuts are, to a certain extent, as in Switzerland, grown all over Europe, but in most countries, such as Germany, Belgium, Holland, etc., the yield is small, and some years not sufficient to supply the home demand, the deficit being supplied from the more favored walnut-growing countries. Thus it will be seen that France, Italy, and Austria-Hungary are the only countries raising that article in sufficient quantities for export.

FRANCE.

The French walnut-growing districts are the departments of Dordogne, Corrèze, Lot, and the Grenoble district, in the department of Isère. The Grenoble nuts are of especially fine quality, being of the soft-shell variety, large, white meat, and running uniformly. These nuts yield the grower from 93 to 105 francs per 100 kilograms (about 8 to 9.18 cents per American pound). The latter price is for Grenoble nuts.

The crop in France this year is good. It compares favorably with former years, and is as good as in 1895. The 1895 crop was above the average, and that of 1894 below.

*Consular Report No. 192, pp. 149–151, September, 1896.

The principal points of export for France are Bordeaux, Marseilles, and Havre.

The trees in France are not subject to scale, blight, or other diseases. The orchards are mostly small and owned by farmers.

ITALY.

The Italian walnut-growing districts are the Neapolitan provinces around Naples, Castellamare di Stabia, and Sorrento. The points of export are Naples and Sorrento.

In Italy, this year's crop compares favorably with former years. Last year's (1895) crop was one fourth less than a medium crop and somewhat inferior to the average.

The principal growing district is Piassio di Sorrento. The trees are, to some extent, owing to climatic influences, subject to scale and blight diseases. The walnuts bring on an average $9 25 per 100 kilograms, or from 4¾ to 5¼ cents per American pound. The extent of orchards is the same as in France.

AUSTRIA-HUNGARY.

The walnut-growing districts of Austria are in the lower part of the empire, or what is known as "Nieder Oestreich." In first line, comes what is known as the Steiermark, where the crop is a medium one; second, Mähren, a good crop; and third, Bosnia, where the crop prospects are excellent. Last year's crop was a light, medium one in the above-named districts, and the nuts, as a rule, are poor, not well filled, small, and of the hard, thick-shelled variety. In Hungary, the districts of Nagy, Bánya, and Grosswardein produce an excellent nut of good quality, large, white meated, and well filled, and, as my informant tells me, compares favorably with the French Marbeaux nuts. No figures as to prices are given.

The point of export for Austria-Hungary is Trieste.

Trees are hardy and not subject to diseases, as scale, etc.

WALNUT EXPORTS TO THE UNITED STATES.

In order that the California walnut-grower may know where he has to look for competition, and what quantities of walnuts are exported to the United States, I have copied and give below the points of shipment and the declared values of walnut exports in dollars (I am unable to get figures as to quantities) to the United States for the last two quarters of the years 1894 and 1895, these being the periods of the year in which walnuts are gathered and shipped, and as given in the United States Treasury returns for the above-named years:

Whence Exported.	1895.	1894.
French.		
Havre	$50,832 39	$12,281 00
Bordeaux	156,579 01	82,282 00
Grenoble district	58,886 00	52,788 00
Marseilles	73,584 00	174,445 00
Italian.		
Castellamare di Stabia	2,624 43	71,809 32
Naples	10,256 00	19,755 85
Sorrento	34,076 00	None.

Austria-Hungary is not credited with any walnut export to the United States. The only other country growing walnuts which exports them to New York and San Francisco that I know of, is Chile. These, as a rule, reach New York and San Francisco in the month of August, and the only data I can find in the United States Treasury returns as to the walnut export from that source is that contained in the returns for the quarter ended September 30, 1894, in which Chile is credited with an export figure of $5,844 48 for that year. No figures are given for 1895, and I presume no walnuts were received.

ZURICH, July 14, 1896.

PLATE X

1.

2.

3.

4.

6.

5.

7.

8.

9.

10.

11.

JUGLANS REGIA, JUGLANS NIGRA, AND JUGLANS SIEBOLDIANA.

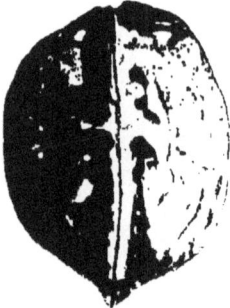

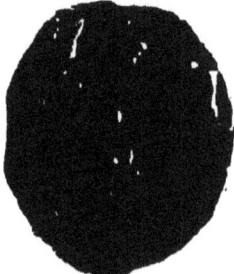

1.

2.

3.

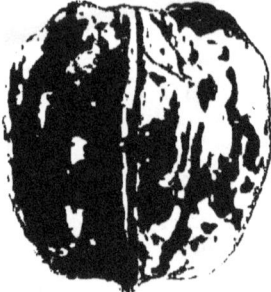

4.

5.

6.

7.

8.

9.

JUGLANS REGIA.

www.ingramcontent.com/pod-product-compliance
Lightning Source LLC
Chambersburg PA
CBHW021629270326
41931CB00008B/932